M.C.

COLOURFUL CHARACTERS
FROM EAST ANGLIA

COLOURFUL
CHARACTERS FROM
EAST ANGLIA

by

H. Mills West

BARBARA HOPKINSON BOOKS

Barbara Hopkinson Books
Heron House
Low Road
Forncett St. Mary
Norwich NR16 1JJ
Tel. 050 841 8367

ISBN 0 9507963 8 7

Printed in England by
Galliard (Printers) Ltd
Great Yarmouth, Norfolk

Contents

Poll and Wideawake	1
Little Dick — Smuggler	7
Cratfield — Parson and Highwayman	16
James Mason — Hermit	22
Henslow of Hitcham — Botanist	28
Alice Driver — Martyr	35
Richard Cobbold — Scribe	42
Rowland Lance — Knight	49
Abraham Cawston — Heir to Millions	57
James Murrell — Wizard	66
Margaret Catchpole — Heroine	72
Marsham — The Tree Man	79
John Elwes — Miser	86
Ted Kittles — Vagrant	93
James Chambers — Compulsive Poet	98
Eleanor Short — Scold	103
Knight and Squire	109
Edward Fitzgerald — Wanderer	115

Poll and Wideawake

They were among the visibly eccentric, these two characters, separated by a century in time but united by a kind
of saintliness in which their entire concern was for their
fellow men. Both were simple countrymen from the same
corner of Suffolk and no doubt both spoke the broad dialect.
John Jacques Steel was a farmer; Horace Reynolds (whom
everyone knew as Poll) was a self-appointed guardian of the
public from traffic driven recklessly through the streets of his
town. Both were known personally or by repute over a wide
area of the county.

Of the two, Poll achieved the more distinguished status
and the larger share of the public's affection, though his role
was a humble one. It would be too facile to describe him as a
traffic warden before his time. His unique place in the
community arose from no consideration of hours and wages
but from an old-fashioned conception of human obligation
and interdependence with one another. Poll was his own
individual and no slot would hold him. Poll was — Poll.
When he died at the age of 32, the whole neighbourhood
wept.

No one seems to know now how Poll came to get this
nickname. It is tempting to call him Old Poll, as no doubt
many did, for this is a term of mild endearment hereabouts.
It is a name that reaches down into the depths of my memory
and I think it must be that Poll was remembered and
mentioned often by my parents in my childhood, for he died
before I was born.

Where he came from, what affliction it was that killed him
and, most important, how it was that this simple young man
made such a deep impression on the people of Woodbridge,
are questions that actual records throw little light on, though
the memorial in the churchyard of St. Mary's does reveal the

extent of the affection in which he was held. It gives this message:

'To the memory of Horace Reynolds (Poll) who died 22nd. August 1910, aged 32 years. Though lacking learning or wealth, by his self-imposed task of watching over motor and other traffic at the Cross Corner in the town, in the course of his duty preventing many serious mishaps, he proved himself a true helper of his fellow men and daily earned the gratitude not only of the townsfolk but also of the motorists and others who passed through the town.

This stone was erected by a number of those who appreciated his services.'

The mention of motor traffic in the years before 1910 indicates the concern at the impact of the new machines upon horse traffic and life generally rather than the volume of vehicles. At that time the automobile had scarcely emerged from the legal constraint of having a man walking ahead with a red flag, but they were noisy, unpredictable things regarded as being of considerable danger to one and all.

It was out of concern for his fellow creatures at the mercy of these unpleasant contraptions and in order to induce some discipline in the horse-drawn traffic in the town, that Poll installed himself, at no one's invitation, at the centre of the Cross Corner. Day after day, in all weathers and whenever there were troubles to be straightened out, Poll would be there. He wore a strange assortment of clothes designed to look like a kind of uniform but with a type of engine driver's cap upon his head and he was armed with a green flag that demanded immediate attention from oncoming drivers.

Despite his odd appearance, there was something completely authoritative about Poll's presence in the midst of the busy crossing and if there were any who laughed at this gaunt figure and his bizarre costume, they were likely to be silenced by the many local citizens who held him in great respect. When Poll died, the whole town mourned as if he had been a member of everyone's family. On the day of the funeral, the bier was carried through the streets, followed by hundreds of people. At the Cross Corner, where the bier rested for a moment at the spot where Poll had supervised so long, the throng of mourners was so great that it was difficult for the bearers to push their way through. Many of those present touched the coffin and openly wept as the concourse moved along Church Street to the churchyard. As Poll had set an example of unselfish help for others so the townsfolk responded in acknowledging their debt of gratitude.

The saintliness of Poll was accentuated by his early death. In the case of John Jacques Steel, the saintliness was markedly absent until he was well into middle age. On the contrary, his early life was of a depraved and vicious kind and, like St. Paul, he was still breathing threats and slaughter when his conversion came in a sudden, blinding flash.

John Jacques was born at Bucklesham, near Ipswich, in 1794, the only son of a well-to-do but profligate tenant farmer. From the beginning, times were hard for the boy. His mother died while he was still an infant and his father could think of no more convenient solution than to send him to a boarding school but a few miles away while he could freely continue his besotted way of life. From the age of seven until eleven John attended the school with none-too-happy holidays at home with his father and then at the tender age of eleven he was pitchforked into heavy farm work. The fact that it was his father's farm made no difference to the harsh treatment he received there at the hands of the farm workers.

'They were a degraded and wicked set of men,' he recalled later in his life. The phrase hints at the unpleasant experiences of a young boy without parental protection thrust into the company of a group of rural oafs and there is no doubt that he was subject to frequent bullying and sexual abuse. Far from having any standing as their employer's son, he received the contempt they felt for his drunken father. With no one to turn to, the boy was seduced into bestial practices and into crime, conspiring with the men to steal

3

from his father's farm.

When John Jacques was eighteen, his father bought a separate farm for him at Walton, near Felixstowe, from the same motive that he had sent him away out of sight to a boarding school. By this time, by his own confession, John Jacques was well down the road to his own kind of debauchery. His marriage to a comely local girl who was to remain a prop and loyal support during all the unpleasant years ahead, retrieved his wild ways for a time but by the age of 22 he had sunk again into the depths of his depraved life. At that time, his weekly visits to Ipswich market commonly lasted for two or three days, during which he drank himself into a stupor in which only the company of the town's basest element suited him.

On occasion he would become embroiled in fights and in his short autobiography he recounts in detail a particular battle he had with one of his own farm men. In a vicious mood against the world generally, he invited the man to have a fight, though with no cause that he could think of save that he wanted to hurt somebody.

The fight did not turn out to John Jacques' advantage, however. The farm hand knocked him down with his first blow and when he got up, without more ado, knocked him down again. John Jacques then retired from the very humiliating lesson he had been given but had spirit enough to go into training with some boxer in Ipswich for the next few weeks. Then, with more confidence, he again challenged the man who had beaten him. This time he remembered all the instructions he had been given about over-coming his opponent quickly in the contest, and impatiently waited for the man to take off his jacket so that he could begin the onslaught. He had barely got his fists up before the man hit him in the eye, a hard blow with bare knuckles. John Jacques went down and did not rise again nor did he ever see again with that eye.

After such episodes, John Jacques returned to his home and family where his wife's unspoken reproach made him more angry than ever from his own remorse and self-

4

contempt. The truth was that he was not by nature evil and the deeper he sank into the mire the more miserable he became. When sober, he hated himself so intensely he only wished to die. Life, in fact, whether his own or another's, seemed of little value. He confessed in his later years that he once planned to take the life of another man but was somehow prevented. When his father died as the result of a fall from his horse when returning home drunk, he could raise no response of pity in himself though he did reflect that this could well be a warning of his own end.

Yet there was still a life that mattered. His young daughter died and now there was no escape from his guilt, even in drink. For the first time he faced the truth, knowing that he had done so little for the child and had even obstructed the mother's care on many occasions. Yet it was said that the child called his name often before she died. With such sobering thoughts he spent the day of the funeral and in the days after continued in a kind of dream in which he scarcely knew the real from the unreal.

Three weeks later, in the same uncertain state of mind, he was riding his horse along a field path on his farm when the miracle happened. As if by its own choice the horse turned aside and entered a woodland path. In the sigh of the wind in the trees he could hear a faint music like the sound of a thousand distant trumpets. As the sound increased, there came a blessed feeling of release and, as he described afterwards, the evil simply fell away from him.

From that day, although there were periods of doubt and difficulty to overcome, John Jacques managed to fight his way to an outright commitment to do good works. Though he saw much of his duty to be crusading evangelism, since he was able to demonstrate the story of his own life as an example of evil overcome, there was side by side with his preaching a real desire to help and comfort those in need.

This however, came only after he had dipped his toes uncertainly in the waters of religion by assisting the local vicar in occasional scripture readings. In his new state of mind such work was soon not enough to satisfy him. He left the established church and joined the Baptists but privately made a reservation that he really belonged to no sect but to the direct teachings of the Bible. Setting out as a free-lance preacher in the neighbourhood of his home, he found very little encouragement and a great deal of opposition especially from established churchmen. He was soon asked what right he had to preach since he had not been ordained and what kind of message could an ex-drunkard give to people, anyway. When he attempted to enter poor-law institutions or hospitals to speak to the inmates, he was often barred by the resident chaplain and on one occasion was escorted away by a policeman.

John Jacques' pulpit, in fact, remained out of doors and ranged the whole length of the beach at Felixstowe, though even here he was frequently jeered and interrupted as he sermonised. The passing years gave him more credence and a kind of tolerance replaced the suspicion eventually as he walked endlessly along the sea-front, almost stumbling along as if his legs could not carry him quick enough. He always dressed in the long black cloak that hid all but his flowing white hair. If people who saw him compared his appearance with that of a John the Baptist, they had some right to do so for this was the Bible figure he admired the most.

From the Ferry end, where he was initially barred from the inn but subsequently received with kindness by the local people, he would hurry along the beach to a meeting below the cliffs or right to the end where the guns of Landguard Fort faced the threat of Napoleon. Under the very walls of the Fort he built a small wooden chapel for the benefit of the soldiers and would hoist a flag when he wanted to begin a service. Perhaps it was the soldiers who first called him Wideawake, since they were bound to give him some nickname and it suited the preacher's constant vigil on the seafront.

For the last fifteen years of his life, John Jacques tried desperately to outweigh the evil of his early life with good works and religious devotion. Whether he succeeded or not is something that could only be decided in the highest court of all.

Little Dick — Smuggler

It is surprising how easily a few generations can span whole centuries of past time and give it all a more familiar aspect. About a dozen very old gentlemen, for example, could in proper sequence bridge the entire period of modern history since the Norman Conquest. In lesser degree, an old person who remembers what he was told in his childhood by another old person looking back at his own childhood, can be recalling over all something of nearly a hundred and fifty years ago. It is in this way that the adventurous deeds of Little Dick, the smuggler, are relayed down to us in scraps and fragments from the lips of old men nursing their pints and their memories in ancient chimney corners. Third hand now, perhaps, from the re-telling, but still warm with the touch of real experience.

In this chain of recollections, the tales come directly from an old man remembering the words of his father, a farm labourer, who in his youth had known the retired smuggler, Charlie Gray. No doubt that the listening youngster would lay up carefully every word that the old reprobate uttered and such words would be repeated exactly so, however long after they were recalled. For that reason these short glimpses of Little Dick's life of adventure as a leader of smugglers along the East Anglian coast must be as authentic as honest memory can make them.

Charlie Gray, the contemporary and friend of Little Dick told the tales when as an old man he would be sitting and taking a measure in a cosy corner of the inn or, if he was not there it was more than likely he'd be at the village smithy. There he would relax, just a comfortable distance from the glowing forge fire, smoking an eccentric mixture of tobacco in a blackened churchwarden pipe and as often as not going over the old days with some old crony. Those who were young would creep up and listen and try to lead him on to tell again the stories of danger and adventure with the smugglers.

'Know Little Dick?' he would say in answer to a frequent question. 'Well, I should say I did! He was a dare-devil if ever there was. People knew his name all along the coast. Always ready to help a friend or shoot an enemy. Oh yes, I knew Little Dick. Afore he was shot and wounded I worked with him many a time. He saved my life more'n once, I can tell you.'

His old eyes would mist over from the sheer surfeit of memories and his listeners would have to wait for a while for him to re-light his pipe with a long spill from the fire.

'What about Little Dick?' he would be urged but there was no hurrying him. He had so many tales to choose from, of fights and chases, of landing contraband on beaches under the very noses of the Excise men and hauling it along country roads at dead of night. He himself had been in many a bloody fight with the Excise.

'Times have changed,' he would say over and over again before he would start on the real adventures. 'You young people can't imagine what it was like being a smuggler in them days. Why, it was organised like an army. Sometimes there'd be two hundred man a-waiting on some beach or at some quiet cove for the goods to come in and there would be a score of waggons and carts to take the stuff away fast to the regular hiding places. I've known six ships come in on a single night at Aldeburgh, carrying tobacco and spirits and going back to Holland with a load of butter. There was money to be had that way for poor people who couldn't earn a mite otherwise.

'Of course, there was some rough customers. Many of us was desperate and that'd go hard for any Excise man to poke his nose in if he was alone. Many a poor chap was done in just for trying to do his duty, but there, the times was hard and smuggling was always an ugly business. Usually, the Excise men would lie low till they could make a raid with a lot of men. Then there'd be hell to pay, fighting hand to hand sometimes, fighting in the dark so you hardly knew friend from foe.

'Of course, there was always danger. You never knew when or where a raid would take place or whether they would bring in the soldiers. When our men was scattered about, the Excise men had the upper hand. They would search the houses and if they found any of the goods they was looking for in your cellar or under your bed you'd be taken off to be tried at the Assizes. They was always trying something new and sometimes we had to take desperate measures to keep the trade going.'

'Even murder?' he was once asked.

'Well,' he replied, after due consideration, 'there was often some shooting and there was fighting with sticks and some men got badly wounded. But I only heard of one deliberate murder. And that was done by strangers — smugglers who came in from Kent. That was the time Little Dick got wounded hisself, shot by one in his own trade. I'll tell you how that happened — but you have to understand first of all what sort of a man Little Dick was.

'He was a man always worked on his own. Not like George Cullum and the other leaders you may have heard of. They sorganised the landings and the paying out of shares to the men and the safe moving of goods to the destined places. But Dick, he'd be here, there and everywhere. No one knew where he'd turn up except that it'd be just when he was needed. He could smell danger and he lived on excitement. Even when he was out of sight you knew he was there nearby and keeping an eye on things. He'd always know if there was going to be a big raid or if some stuff should be moved quickly to some new hiding place. If there was danger or the whisper of danger he'd be there. Trouble? Wherever there was trouble or the threat of trouble that's where Little Dick would be, all of a sudden with his big black horse steaming and lathering and pistols in his hands. That was Little Dick. Little? Why, he was six foot tall and as strong as an ox.

'Oh, yes, I knew Little Dick well enough. He and I had many a narrow escape together and many dealings on dark

9

nights along the coast. A score of times I'd see him astride of his black horse just quietly standing among the sand dunes or in the shadow of some trees. That horse of his was the best that I ever did see. It looked as if it could ride through the eye of a needle or take wings and fly over a haystack. It was called Prince and a prince it certainly turned out to be. It saved my life once and its master's many a time.

'There was one night that I remember well. The Excise chaps knew there was a specially big load coming in and they called in the soldiers, the Dragoons who were armed with muskets and had orders to use them if necessary. Somehow, Little Dick got wind of the soldiers coming but it was too late to stop the boats or to warn the men waiting to unload. I was just about to join the others on the beach when he came galloping like the wind across the heath.

' "Don't go down to the cove, Charlie," he shouted. "There's a hundred soldiers a-following. We've got to lead them away."

'I rode beside Dick, looking like a poor relation on my old pony, and he seemed in no great hurry until the foremost of the soldiers came into view. Then he turned his horse northward away from the landing beach and rode like mad as if in a panic to warn his mates farther along.

' "Look after yourself, Charlie," he shouted. There was no keeping up with him. I turned aside into the thicket and the troop of soldiers galloped past without interest although they must have seen me. The fact of it was that they had recognised Little Dick — as he meant them to do — and with a high price on his head they were only interested in the glory of capturing such a notorious outlaw.

'That night, I learned afterwards, he led them a fine dance across country. The soldiers had no knowledge of the area and somehow Dick managed to get them so far away from the coast and danger as to reach Easton, near Wickham Market. There was no catching that horse and the Dragoons had little chance of loading and firing their muskets. Dick would have got clear away but for a piece of bad luck. When he reached the river he found it swollen with the rains and

10

sweeping along in a torrent. There was no time for hesitation but for a moment as they plunged in he prayed to the good Lord to forgive him for putting Prince to such a heavy struggle. But as if he knew just what was wanted of him, old Prince swam and fought his way slantwise across the channel, dragging Little Dick along at the side holding on to the saddle out of sight of the soldiers. In the end, they landed safely and found a friendly hiding place on a farm where Dick had often delivered merchandise. It turned out well enough but it was a near thing that night.

'Dick laughed about it afterwards. Always happy after a bit of excitement, he was. Never much concerned about the profits provided he got his share of the adventure. I can tell you there was many a time when I was glad to know that Little Dick was not far away. But for him I'd be as dead as mutton now instead of sitting here talking to you. I got too close to the business end of a pistol one night and he — but there, I'll tell you how that all come about.

'I'd been visiting old Tom Warren where he lived in what we called the sandlings there just above Woodbridge. That was harvest time and a lovely evening and it seemed as good a time as any to go and pay Tom for the cheese and the butter firkins that he'd got for me by the usual route. Well, we were sitting there talking and smoking and sampling a keg of very good brandy until well after midnight. After all, we'd been confederates and good friends for years and we had a good laugh, remembering some of the tricks we'd been up to together.

'When I set off for home it was bright moonlight. I had to follow a track through the trees where it was quiet and shadowy but I knew the area well and had no trouble following the path. In time I came out on to the main road and as soon as I got there I could hear the rumbling of carts coming down the hill. There was no doubt what those carts would be carrying, there and at that time of night and not much doubt either who would be riding close by as the convoy moved along.

'Little Dick, I thought, Little Dick for a farthing! And I

11

remembered I wanted to see him to ask him about leaving me a tub or two of rum for Michaelmas. I waited at the side of the road till the convoy come up. Well, perhaps I'd had a drop too much of Tom Warren's contraband rum that night to make me do something so reckless. Usually I was as careful as a cat. But just as the foremost waggon come abreast of me I walked out into the road and called Dick's name. There was no answer from Dick but the waggon stopped suddenly and the huge figure of a man in a great sea-cloak and a sou-wester showed up in the moonlight. In an instant he had a horse-pistol in his hand, resting on the rail of the cart and pointed straight at my head. I really believed that was my last moment on earth.

'Then — "Hold!" someone shouted. "Hold your fire!" It was Little Dick. His black horse came dashing out of the shadows of the trees. The sailor with the horse pistol hesitated as if he still had a mind to blow my head off, then, swearing and grumbling, edged back into the cart.

' "You damned fool, Charlie," Little Dick shouted. "Another second and you'd have gone to Kingdom Come. There's Dutch sailors on this trip and ready to shoot anybody who stops them."

'Well, that was the narrowest escape I ever had and all because of my own stupidity. Lucky for me that night that Little Dick was close by. But I was going to tell you about the time Little Dick himself got wounded. Shot, he was, and all on account of trying to rescue an Excise man from the Kentish smugglers. It was a long time afore he was in action again with our lot.

'That happened later the same year, October time, on a Sunday morning when a great mob of Kentish men landed up near Sizewell. We were no friends of the Kentish lot, I can tell you. They caused us a heap of trouble one way and another, pushing their way into what we regarded as being our own backyard. But they was a real tough lot. That day they put ashore with a big cargo of tobacco and spirits and somehow got horses to carry the stuff inland. They was strong enough and cocksure enough to march along in broad

12

daylight and no one daring to lift a finger to stop them. They went right along to Beccles like a regular little army, then to Bungay and down to Harleston, dropping off their goods on the way.

'Of course, we knew what was happening and we could be sure that Little Dick would be keeping a close eye on the mob and where they unloaded the stuff. What we didn't know was that the Kent men were here to do murder. They were looking for one particular man, an Excise officer named Mr. Brock who had arrested some of their pals a month or two earlier and they were dead-set on revenge.

'They must have spent the Sunday night like gipsies in the open somewhere in the Harleston area then next day made off to the south-west, just following the gossip and the directions of people they come across. After a long trek, the gang reached the village of Yaxley about mid-day. It wasn't long before they found Mr. Brock, who happened to be taking his usual mug of ale at the inn there. There was nothing that the landlord or the locals could do when the mob burst in and dragged the Excise man out into the open, nor did anyone feel tempted to interfere when they beat him up in broad daylight. Then they put him on one of their horses and got ready to leave. There was no doubt about what would happen to him on their way back to the coast.

'Little Dick had followed the Kent mob most of the way but after putting up for the night at a wayside inn had lost the trail next morning. It was not until the smugglers were just setting off from Yaxley that he caught up with them again. He could see at a glance what was happening but it was touch and go whether he would interfere, he told me later. Well, of course it would have been better to think twice in a situation like that but Dick was always one for action rather than meditation. No matter that Mr. Brock was a natural enemy and a man who was personally disliked by everyone in our trade, the idea of cold-blooded murder committed by a rival trader right in the middle of our own territory made him lose all regard for his own safety and determine to rescue the man.

13

'The first the smugglers knew of his presence was when Prince came thundering towards them with Little Dick bent low over the horse's neck and a pistol in his hand pointed at any who tried to stop him. In the immediate confusion he managed to grasp the reins of the horse carrying Mr. Brock and almost managed to get him away, what with the surprise of the attack and the stupidity of the smugglers, but he had scarcely got twenty yards before one of them recovered his senses and fired. If Dick had been on Prince alone, he would have been away and gone but leading the other horse with an injured man in the saddle brought a hopeless drag to the escape. The ball hit Dick in the right arm. It brought him down crashing at the side of the road and the mob hurriedly collected the Excise man's mount and moved away. A man shot near a main road could bring a hue and cry and the gang had a long way to go to get back to their ship.

'Well, Dick's big black horse, Prince, was not hurt and he was standing quietly by as local people came out from the cottages and see Dick there trying to staunch his wound. There was plenty of folk ready to look after him, for all that he was known to be a leader of smugglers, for there were not many who had not benefited from his activities in the past.

'As for Mr. Brock, nothing was ever heard of him again. Soldiers were brought in to search the whole area of the route that the smugglers must have taken on their way back to Sizewell but they found nothing. No doubt the mob found it more convenient to drop the man overboard after they was at sea.

'That was a bad time all round. Trouble with the Kentish lot, trouble to come from the Excise as sure as anything could be and trouble because Little Dick was no longer there to keep our spirits up. I made up my mind then to get out of the smuggling trade as soon as I could manage it. I had to be careful because there was many in that brotherhood who'd take very unkindly to people who backed out, in case they were tempted to name names. Not many years before a man who'd been one of the regular runners for most of his life got suddenly sick of the business and wanted to give it up.

Somehow the Excise people managed to persuade him that he should go to London and give full evidence to the authorities. He was foolish enough to agree but on his journey to London got no further than Ipswich where he was murdered. There was no evidence about who had committed the murder but it was common sense to add up the score and add that deed to the many crimes of the fraternity,

'In the end, I retired to this here village away from the old smuggling haunts and I've been quite happy to forget them days. One thing I couldn't forget was Little Dick and I heard from time to time how he recovered from his wound and how he got back to lead the lads again. But after a great raid just south of Lowestoft that night when hundreds of soldiers were brought in to smash the trade, I heard no more. I think he was taken. It upset everything for a time and Little Dick just seemed to have vanished. I believe he must have been taken in that battle or he was wounded and was swept out to sea. I don't know, nor what happened to Prince, in the end. They're thoughts that I don't dwell on nowadays.'

Charlie would sink into silence then and finger his pipe and look deep into the forge fire. For all his professed relief at living out his old age in the peace and security of this village, it was easy to tell how much he yearned sometimes for the old days. They had formed the substance and the reality of his life and what remained was a shadow, a mere epilogue to a thrilling drama played to the accompaniment of galloping hooves along windy cliff-tops long ago.

Cratfield —
Parson and Highwayman

From the first day of his ordination, the new rector succeeded in offending his parishioners and raising something like consternation among the immediate circle of the faithful. His ways were not those expected of an accredited parson no matter how broadminded the village flock and protests were soon on their way to the bishop, who wisely let the matter rest for the moment.

The parish of Wortham, near Diss, could not have been more charmingly rustic and undemanding of a new incumbent. Indeed, a certain latitude was always given to the clergy there in the expectation of minor eccentricities arising as a right from their superior education and incomes. The new rector was apparently endowed quite generously with both these gifts, having two livings instead of one and an impressive academic background. He could have easily filled the role assigned to a parish priest by long precept as a slightly idiosyncratic, unworldly interpreter of the scriptures. It was not a difficult part to play. Parishioners were upset to find that he did not comfortably fit into any such prescribed place or indeed into the rustic life of Wortham at all. He came like a wolf to the sheep-fold, like a satyr among the innocent, the man who called himself William Baret de Cratfield and claimed to be descended from the first Norman settlers. Not many people in the village cared for the French part of the name. To them and to the host of people to whom the rector was to become only too well known, William Cratfield was name enough.

'We must give hime time to settle down', the bishop insisted, in answer to the initial complaints. After all, country people often got themselves locked into certain familiar patterns of thought and they were bound to be prejudiced against any new face and any new ways. Not everyone could fill the shoes of that benign and much-loved rector who was his predecessor and a new-comer would seem to have rough edges and strange manners to begin with. Nevertheless, the bishop was concerned enough to have a few words with the Abbot of St. Edmundsbury in whose patronage the living of Wortham lay. Together they sent a short and friendly message to the Rev. Cratfield, advising him that some of his actions and utterances were offending devout church-goers. They hoped he would allow for rural insularity and take a more moderate and indulgent attitude.

Obviously, the message had little effect. As the months passed, so local indignation mounted. The rector's total disdain of proper forms of worship, of pastoral duties and the feelings of conscientious church workers, brought the matter again and again to the notice of the bishop and the patron. A quiet investigation showed that the complaints were justified, even under-stated. In the last resort, when Cratfield had proved that he was not likely to mend his ways, the prelates brought their joint pressure upon him to resign. At first rebellious and openly contemptuous both of his masters and of his flock, the situation became so tense with ill-feeling that in the end the rector had to yield. On the day that Cratfield left the village the locals celebrated with a bonfire on the green where a roughly-made effigy of a man in a dog-collar was consigned to the flames. What was to happen to the rector and where he would go was something that no one knew and very few people cared. Even less were they likely to be concerned about what effect the dismissal would have upon the cleric. It was simply a matter of common relief that he was gone from the parish.

In fact, the Rev. Cratfield seemed to sink immediately into the kind of obscurity he so richly deserved. Nothing was heard of him for a period of some months and then there were only whispers and rumours, tales told third-hand about the man and his new way of life.

In those days, the heaths around Newmarket were

notorious as the resort of cut-throats and thieves, for it not only provided the perfect setting for the ambushing of unfortunate travellers but also an effective hiding place from the law. Even though some of the robbers were known by name to the authorities, it was only on a rare occasion when a capture could be made and an offender brought to justice. So it was that when respectable citizens had to travel in that area by coach they left their valuables at home and prayed that they would be allowed to reach their destinations without the loss of more than a few sovereigns to the human jackals who were almost certain to be lying in wait. And those who prayed added an urgent supplication that if they should be held up by anyone, it would not be the infamous cut-throat, William Cratfield, Rector of Wortham. For this was the new profession of the former churchman, and one at which he was to become spectacularly successful.

Cratfield carried out his regular and vicious atrocities upon travellers with the aid of only one companion, since he would trust no one else. This henchman was a slight and cowardly man named Thomas Tapyrestone (sometimes Tepytrone), a failed hosier by trade with a grudge against society but without the strength of purpose to do much protesting himself. Under Cratfield's wing he showed his dubious character in supporting his chief without exposing himself to too much danger. Nor did the parson over-estimate the value of his assistant, giving him little more importance than he would give to a well-trained dog. Nevertheless, there was enough mutual benefit in the association to keep the two miscreants together through several years of crime of a kind which was recounted with awe and sent respectable people shuddering to their beds.

The heathland was Cratfield's empire. For many years he reigned over the whole area, exacting homage from lesser crooks, taking the pick of the loot and eluding all attempts at capture. After nine years on the heath, he decided to try his fortune in London itself, where there were sure to be richer hauls to be made. The fact that it would be more dangerous only added to the excitement. In any case, the mass of ill-lit

18

streets and complex alley-ways would partly discount the close proximity of the law and it would be a simple and profitable exercise to way-lay unwary pedestrians and then quickly disappear.

It soon became known that Cratfield had changed his hunting-ground and special efforts were made to track down the notorious footpad but all in vain. He could disappear in the maze of London streets as swiftly as ever he had done on Newmarket heath. As his ambitions soared, so the number and scale of the robberies increased, his victims chosen from among the wealthier of the city. Among these unfortunates was a goldsmith, a Mr. Bottomer, who was ill-advised enough to walk home regularly through the alley-ways that at that time existed in Faringdon.

That night the two ruffians were waiting, knowing the route that the goldsmith would take and the exciting probability that he would be actually carrying some gold bullion on his person. Mr. Bottomer was an easy prey, quickly yielding up some £12 in gold and the contents of his pockets, realising that with these desperate rogues and in that benighted part of the city, he was entirely at the mercy of the pair. Had the robbery taken place on Newmarket heath the goldsmith may well have lost his life also but here perhaps the chance of a hue-and-cry made the rogues more cautious of inflicting physical harm. Mr. Bottomer was allowed to go on his way. His freedom was to spell the beginning of the downfall of the miscreants.

As soon as he had recovered from his ordeal, Mr. Bottomer laid a complaint before the authorities with a full description which allowed them to identify the assailants and issue an official notice of the crime:

'William Cratfield, late rector of the church of Wortham in Norfolk and Thomas Tepytrone, late of London, hosier of the parish of St. Leonard, in the ward of Faringdone, did feloniously rob one William Bottomer, goldsmith, on the 28th May in the fourth year of the reign of our Sovereign Lord the King, taking £12 in gold and the ready money upon him.'

Upon this notice, a jury was engaged to indict the two men, despite the fact that they were still at liberty. Accordingly, a verdict was passed in their absence finding the pair guilty of treason and felony. Writs were issued for their arrest. All that was needed now was to catch them.

It proved to be a long and frustrating process. The court sheriff, armed with a writ, could call on a veritable posse to help him track down the wanted pair but only within his own bailiwick. Such a restriction was very much to Cratfield's taste and it was soon obvious that he had skipped to pastures new, where the process of issuing a writ would have to be gone through all over again. For two years Cratfield took a fiendish delight in the game of hide-and-seek among the wards of London until in despair the authorities designated him 'exigent'. This meant that the parson had the alternative of giving himself up to the court for trial or being officially posted as an outlaw. It was a move that must have caused Cratfield to pull up sharply and consider his position. As an outlaw he could still evade the authorities — he had always done so and the fact of being an outlaw made capture no easier — but he realised that danger could come from within the fraternity. An outlaw could be caught and hanged in the manner of a lynching without any questions asked and there were many among the fraternity who were jealous of Cratfield's standing and would gladly seek an opportunity to betray him while suffering no harm to themselves.

In keeping with his past record and the spite which he seemed to feel towards the whole world, Cratfield chose to become an outlaw and take the consequences upon his own head. He returned at once to the Newmarket heathland with Tapyrestone still in attendance and their presence was soon marked by a period of unremitting violence towards unfortunate travellers. Increasing jealousies among the fraternity and more frequent visits to the area by searching Sheriff's men made the next few months uneasy ones for the pair and it must have occurred to both that the weight of circumstances was turning against them. Inevitably, the time would come when they would be caught and little justice beyond a length of rope could they expect. Cratfield aggravated the worsening situation by forming an alliance with a young woman for whom he showed all the signs of an infatuation. Tapyrestone immediately recognised the danger that lay in such an association and decided to cut loose from the long-standing partnership. It was a move that brought him little reward however, for on joining up with a band of lesser brigands, he was soon after betrayed to the Sheriff and captured. Cratfield apparently besotted by his feelings for his lady friend, allowed his crony to depart without any concern but he soon regretted the loss. Without the eyes and ears of the ever-vigilant Tapyrestone, who for all his faults had been a devoted watch-dog, Cratfield quickly became vulnerable to the many forces out to get him by one means or another. For the first time, his judgments were impaired by emotion and the very presence of the woman posed an encumbrance when speed and decision were required. He discovered this to his cost when brought to the final chase across the heathland with a posse in hot pursuit. Alone, he might have escaped as he had done so many times before, but the woman had no experience of such desperate circumstances and would have been soon left behind but that he refused to leave her. He was taken at last and removed to Newgate with the woman.

Behind the prison doors the one-time clergyman languished for some weeks in the company of thieves and vagabonds of disrepute and occasionally of his mistress before reaping the punishment deemed suitable for his misdemeanours. A short paragraph of news recorded the facts:

'A parson of Wortham, in Norfolk, who has haunted Newmarket Heath for some time, robbing and despoiling many of the King's subjects, was now, with his concubyne, brought into Newgate, where he died.'

The announcement errs on the side of under-statement. Cratfield died indeed, but violently at the hands of the hangman.

James Mason — Hermit

If hermits were judged by the amount of publicity they inspired, then the Mason brothers would surely win first prize. People at home in East Anglia or in far-flung places abroad have read of them and perhaps wondered why the couple have merited such attention. As hermits, per se, they were not all that meritorious. Tommy was perhaps no more than one third of a hermit, as hermits go, and the invisible but ever-watchful Jimmy about two thirds of an out-and-out anchorite. Yet a number of reasons have caused the lives of these two men, particularly that of Jimmy, to be wondered at and conjured into a kind of legend. With time and sustained public curiosity they may well become as famous as the Brontes of Hawarth.

Tommy and Jimmy Mason lived in the village of Great Canfield in Essex, until their middle years with their mother, in the family house named Sawkins. Unfortunately, there were frequent quarrels between the two brothers and Jimmy set out to build his own separate dwelling on the same four-acre holding but as far as possible from the main house. For some years after it was completed, Jimmy spent only the days at the timber hut which he called New Place, returning to the family home for meals and to sleep. He devoted a great deal of time and energy working on New Place, fortifying it as if for a siege. In the end it was almost inaccessible, with a mound and moat on one side, a high hedge and pond fronting the road and with all approaches from within the holding baulked by a complex arrangement of barbed wire and wild undergrowth.

Add to this the remoteness of the Mason's piece of land and the narrow, muddy lanes that led to it and a more complete hermitage can hardly be imagined. But for the curiosity of a local newspaper man, Jimmy could well have spent his life here with no one hearing a word about him. As it was, with interesting local news being scarce at the time, he was suddenly revealed as a man who had renounced the world for the sake of a lost love. It was a story too good to leave to the local press and it was soon embellished by Fleet Street with touches of tear-jerking tenderness. If it did not make the public actually beat a muddy path to Jimmy's door, it certainly aroused a considerable amount of curiosity.

'Wild Man of the Woods' was the headline in the *Daily Mail*. 'Jilted in Love, Seeks Balm in Seclusion.'

'Alone in a plantation at Great Cranfield, Essex, lives a wild man in the prime of life. Thirteen years ago he loved a woman but she jilted him and, vowing never to look on a female's face again, he plunged into the woods to live — to brood and sigh for the love he had lost.'

Jimmy was probably more surprised than anybody at being given such a romantic background, though in fact he was certainly not immune to the charms of the opposite sex for whom he felt a deep but necessarily distant regard. The extent to which a hermit can have an association with a young woman, while remaining a committed hermit, is limited. Yet somehow, during his long years at New Place, Jimmy achieved a situation in which, without ever speaking or being clearly seen by anyone, he kept up a kind of relationship with village children and a succession of young maidens with a remarkable degree of success. For some time Jimmy kept a diary in which the development of this strange rapport was fully described, showing how he was able to maintain a considerable influence over the local children while remaining mysteriously out of sight, by making regular offerings of small gifts. It was easily achieved to begin with because of the proximity of the pond to the road. He would throw apples, nuts, or greengages over the high hedge into the pond for the children to recover.

When this novel distribution of largesse became known to the children they would often meet at the pond to find what was currently on offer. Sometimes they shouted to the shadowy figure beyond the hedge, on occasion the naughtier of the boys would throw stones, but sometimes too, the girls would speak 'tenderly', knowing that the hermit would not hurt anyone. Commerce in the summer months increased, with Jimmy putting gifts on the rail of the gate or in the fork of the nearby tree — usually eggs, or packets of money, with vegetables, fruit and nuts as they came in season. The modest offerings were always put out in the late evening after dark when he could not be seen and when he thought that Tommy and his mother had gone to bed. He would go out two or three times afterwards to check if the things were gone.

In this way, the hermit managed to obtain an extraordinarily detailed knowledge of the children. Their conversations were often repeated in full in his diary, together with their names (usually wrongly spelt) and even their ages and how they were dressed. He was particularly fascinated by two or three young girls who came to join in this mute but profitable kind of communication. With these, as he became bolder, he would sometimes exchange notes. The messages were always of a most prosaic kind and placed and received through the good offices of the fir-tree near the gate. There is no doubt that in his way he felt some fondness for two or three of the girls for he showed some irritation at seeing them walk out with village boys. Perhaps it was a whisper of this that caused the local newspapers to write of Jimmy as a rejected lover.

His concern for Edna, for example, was constant but ever remote, always observing rather than participating. On occasion, Edna would go off for a visit to London. On returning she might or might not put a note in the tree for Jimmy but if she did it would be one in which money largely figured. He would often put money out for her, but only in small amounts. 'Things put out on rail at half past nine,' he would record in his diary. 'Found not gone two or three times. All gone quarter to eleven. Was 2s, eggs, ripe apples and radish.'

In early September, Jimmy observed Edna keeping a rendezvous with a strange young man and used a telescope to watch them walking together. An hour or two later she came running excitedly by New Place as she returned from the outing. She was carrying her hat, noted the ever-watchful Jimmy and 'she seemed as if so pleased'.

Jimmy was not so pleased. The following Saturday he left plums, apples, eggs and 1s. 3d. on the rail as well as a letter asking what the man had wanted there. Apparently there was no reply and the next Sunday Edna came past dressed in her best as if for an assignation but Jimmy could not spy the man anywhere. However, the following Sunday Edna again walked past. Jimmy wrote: 'Edna going by again to meet the man. Had best red things on. She went into large pasture by wood.'

At the beginning of October, Jimmy put out his gifts as usual. When he went out later to see if they had been taken, he found a note from Edna in the basket. 'Said she wanted 10s. to buy a cloak for winter. Said the man about the wood so many Sundays was only her cousin Jack. She only went round wood with him to pick nuts.'

Jimmy duly put out some fruit and a small amount of money on the gate for Edna but was displeased when Sunday came and Edna went by in her best red clothes. She glanced rather guiltily towards New Place as if knowing the hermit would be watching. 'And it was directly she got round the corner that a man went round after her, walking so fast.'

However, Jimmy could easily be twisted around Edna's little finger. In November another letter of excuses came. 'Said had no shoes and wanted money to buy some, else she would never write another letter!'

Jimmy's generosity was being tested to the utmost at that time since it was a period of great poverty for the Masons. Tommy was angry with Jimmy for giving away money when it was so badly needed and sometimes tried to drive the children away by rattling a pail loudly with a stick. One night when Jimmy had put the offerings on the rail he went out later to find 'that raskle' Tommy hiding under a bush with the loot he had recovered. Jimmy had had the utmost suspicion of Tommy ever since the day he had gone up to the main house, taken a pudding from the larder for his evening meal and found it intolerably bitter. After eating only a mouthful, he gave the rest to his dog which immediately showed signs of acute poisoning and was dead within an hour. He himself felt desperately ill all next day.

Jimmy grieved deeply over his dog. 'Poor little thing, never to bark any more,' he wrote and when he found that Tommy had buried the dog he dug it up again and gave it a solemn funeral in a chosen spot. He believed that this was a deliberate attempt on his life though both Tommy and his mother declared the pudding to be wholesome. He also believed that Tommy had poisoned their father and certainly Tommy never disguised his acute hatred for the man who had caused the brothers so much childhood misery. Even in his old age he would burst forth with bitter recriminations and frequently express the wish that his father had died sooner.

Both Tommy and Jimmy had cause for resentment. Their father was a long-serving army man, leaving the service at the age of 45 with the rank of serjeant. He continued to be a martinet of the fiercest kind within his own family, visiting on his two sons an excessive discipline demanding unquestioning obedience and often physical hardship. What actually happened to the boys within the home people could only guess but they could see clearly the kind of iron-fisted treatment the boys received out of doors. This included being marched to church on Sundays in silence and in step and extended to occasionally putting the boys out of the house at night and not allowing them in until the morning. It would not be difficult, I imagine, to associate all the repressions of their later lives with the cruelty of their childhood. For some reason, Jimmy seemed able to forgive more readily than Tommy, for when his brother came out with some vilification, he would acidly apportion his parents in the pages of his diary: 'his mother, my father.'

Jimmy's remote love affair with the local young people continued with Fanny and Lily and Gertrude and the others but it was supposed to be Susie to whom the invisible man's heart really called out. It was said that from the earliest days Jimmy had trained his dog to follow Susie with a note fastened to its collar and it would not go away until she had taken it. Jimmy would often be about in the fields after dark when he could not be seen and when Susie started work outside the village and had to walk back to her home at night she could sometimes feel that he was following close behind. There was one night when she started to run and he followed, calling out the only words he had ever been heard to utter by anyone other than his brother and his mother. She was not to run, he told her soothingly, not to feel frightened for it was only her sweetheart that followed her.

In her turn, Susie's sister Fanny availed herself of Jimmy's gifts and showed herself to be blatantly acquisitive. The few notes that passed between them dealt solely with the commerce at the gate and Jimmy directed that the pick of the produce should be taken and given to his favourite Susie. Fanny may well have carried out this chore in order to please Jimmy, for she was intent on obtaining a more substantial present before she left the village. 'If you do not give me a watch and chain X X X X there will never be a Miss Fanny if you do not give me a watch and chain X X X X. I do so much like a watch and I like a chain.'

Despite the growing debts and the worries about having to give up the Sawkins holding, Jimmy eventually managed to give Fanny her watch and chain. It marked the climax of the strange, half-tender, half-querulous magnanimity of the unseen hermit at the trysting-place beside the pond.

Jimmy died in solitude at the age of 84, having been a confirmed recluse for 60 years. Towards the end of his life a woman from the village was asked to go daily to the hut to help care for the old man. Jimmy took the visits sourly and had little to say except to tell her that if she came one day and found the door open and his boots outside, she would know that he was dead. That, indeed, was exactly what she found.

Henslow of Hitcham — Botanist

It was not, to begin with, a matter of earth-shaking importance to the local population when the new parson arrived to take up his duties in the village of Hitcham in 1837. If the event was noted at all it was with some sardonic amusement from the farmers of the area, while the labouring families were so lost in the apathy of drudgery that they barely lifted their heads to greet him. They had seen new parsons before. The last one had come to the village with fine ideas about helping the cottagers to improve their lot and he had beaten his head valiantly against the brick wall of the farmers' interests. In the end, he had had to retreat, completely disillusioned and spiritless. If this new parson had such high-flying notions about improving labouring conditions, he'd soon be on the way out, too.

For his part, the Rev. Henslow marked the sullen faces and the signs of poverty and oppression, no less acute for all the verdant beauty of the area. He watched the diminutive figures of children working in the fields and saw how the wives struggled with the domestic tyranny of a small cottage and a large family that must be fed and somehow cared for. These people lived in a blind tunnel of hopelessness, he perceived, in which there was no way out but old age and death. In their situation where jobs, homes and freedom lay in the hands of the powerful farmers, there could not be a man foolhardy enough not to accept whatever hours and conditions his employer prescribed. There would not be a wife who dared to resist working in the fields when required nor risk being noted as absent from church on any Sunday morning. Nor would any child's protests earn him respite from the stone-picking and crow scaring for twopence a day. It was the traditional way of the labouring life. A parson more or less could make no difference to the established scheme of things.

Had they known that the Rev. Henslow was a man of stature in the world, a Professor who lectured at Cambridge University, who chaired learned societies and held a national reputation as a scientist, it would have made little difference to local opinion. Such high-sounding qualifications only made the gulf that much wider and the understanding so much less. The Professor should go back to his clever friends at the University and so far as any one in the village was concerned, the sooner the better. In the wildest dreams of the most imaginative cottager was it ever considered possible that in twenty years this unassuming man would bring fame and learning to the village, transform the lives of labourers and provide hope and confidence to all who lived within its boundaries?

There is a kind of illogical persistence about reformers of Henslow's stature that puts them in a separate group, a kind of awkward squad that doesn't know when it is beaten. It would have been a sensible action on his part to have washed his hands of the place and departed. After all, there was no doubt about the kind of welcome that the farming fraternity offered. One gentleman made it quite clear in a letter to the Rector: 'I am sorry to say that it appears you are one of those philanthropical gentlemen who wish to make themselves popular with the lower class of society at the expense of the farmer.' This was an indignant reaction to Henslow's unheard-of idea of providing the cottagers with allotments.

From the first, Henslow had battles to fight that were heavily weighted against him and it is to his credit that he shirked none of them. His position was particularly difficult since he was an ordained clergyman putting forward the cause of science in the very thick of the high feeling that existed in rural areas against the monstrous idea of evolution. Stubborn ignorance and prejudice faced him at all times and, strangely enough, seemed to rouse in him an even greater determination to help them despite themselves. It became a cause beside which his distinguished duties as

Fellow, Professor, Tutor to the Royal Children and his scientific studies all seemed comparatively unimportant. He saw in Hitcham a microcosm of the whole problem of rural life and to that small village he devoted most of his energies and much of his fortune.

What must he do first? Perhaps first of all just to make friends with the labouring families, try to make them understand that he cared for their plight and believed that there were ways by which their hardship could be alleviated. A contemporary journal described some of Henslow's efforts in this direction: 'He invited them to the Rectory lawn in the evening and amused them with fireworks and then gradually introduced to their notice many simple objects of domestic use hitherto unknown to them and having once gained their confidence he lost no time in setting to work on a plan that should tell at once on the bodies and minds of the labourers.'

This was the typical Henslow approach — a spoonful of sugar to help the medicine go down. He often wrote to distinguished friends at Cambridge to ask them to send him quantities of sweets, which duly served their purpose of helping small tongues to loosen and talk to him freely. Looming ahead were the real problems that he intended to tackle and overcome one by one. First, help for the poorest families and advice on using their wages to best advantage. Then a piece of land, an allotment that every able-bodied man could work for his own benefit. Most of all a school for all the children and reading lessons for adults so that they should not feel left out. In the school would be set up a botany class where the young would learn to see and understand more thoroughly the countryside around them. Then there would be ploughing matches and annual flower shows and expeditions for everyone to join. It was a brave programme. Henslow knew well that each one of these projects would be hindered and baulked with the utmost venom by all the powerful farmers and gentry around.

Since he could do nothing about raising the low wages himself, he pursuaded the poorer villagers to organise their spending to better advantage. Before long there was a coal club, a childrens' clothing club, a medical club and a ploughing match club. Henslow hoped that these simple projects would be helped along by contributions from the better-off, but very little cash materialised beyond that from the Rector's own purse. There was similar resistance when Henslow introduced the idea of ploughing matches as an interest for the men, since it was feared the labourers would get above themselves. There was also the excuse that farms whose ploughmen lost the competition would suffer in reputation. As for allotments, no farmer had land to spare for such a hare-brained scheme and it was not until Henslow was able to buy 16 acres of Charity Land himself that the enthusiastic spade-work began. Fortunately, there were a number of interested people outside the village who came up with gifts of seeds, organic manure and cutting tools to help the project.

Since this parson seemed to be capable of anything likely to undermine traditional village life, there was a kind of bemused but mounting indignation when he turned his attention to the building of a schoolroom. In fact, this was Henslow's main ambition, the founding of a local school. From the beginning he had been completely dedicated to the idea from which so many benefits could flow. Illiteracy and the resulting ignorance he saw as the greatest bugbear of rural life. All other important assignments at Cambridge and elsewhere were put aside until the school was built and a schoolmistress installed. He appealed to the employers again to help in raising the funds necessary but with little result. Hoping there were a few of a more liberal turn of mind among them, Henslow astutely reminded them of the principles of Self Help, then a popular movement among the more enlightened. There was a small response. Again he sent out a letter, in which the appeal was disguised by quoting the words of well-known people who had spoken out against the meanness of some villages towards their poor.

Subscriptions for the school gradually rose. Two years

after it opened there were 40 rough and ragged pupils in the classroom, adequately provided for by a total sum of £26, including the childrens' own daily pence. Next year, by some miracle of persuasion, there were 90 voluntary pupils in the instruction of a single teacher. Henslow, using every device to keep subscriptions coming in from unwilling farmers, was driven to using the pulpit and his sermonizing eloquence to further what he regarded as a fitting God's cause.

Grumbles became louder. This parson not only wanted healthy youngsters to sit down and do nothing all day in school but was talking of classes for their parents as well. No matter that the school had been officially examined, approved and blessed with a modest grant, the sheer waste of young labour and the likelihood that cottage children would learn ideas above their own station, were thoughts hard to come to terms with. It was the last straw when the Professor inaugurated what was to him the high point of the whole exercise — a botany class.

In these days such an innovation seems to be a matter of complete unimportance. At that time, the subject of science was a sore point with the faithful, who saw it as opposing the basics of religious belief. The study of plants and animals in particular seemed to be a pastime for the ungodly. That an ordained minister should so forget his faith as to wantonly institute a class to study botany was beyond endurance. Perhaps local feeling would have been more outraged if it had been known that the despised Charles Darwin had been a pupil of Henslow's at Cambridge and that only family commitments had prevented the Professor from leading that fateful expedition to the Galapagos Islands himself.

Henslow felt the storm about him but saw nothing that was contradictory in his position. When he gave an address at the opening of the Ipswich Natural History Museum, he explained his own view: 'If they (his critics) tell me that science is necessarily a snare and an obstruction to spiritual progress, I tell them in return that I utterly deny and disbelieve their assertions.' Understanding nature scientifically, he believed, only strengthened faith in a divine creator.

At all events, nothing deterred the Rector from his enthusiastic experiment in teaching botany to the children of his country parish. As it turned out, it was a project of such success as to win national acclaim and widespread imitation. Much credit was given to the Professor for dedicating his energies and teaching skills to the furtherance of this botany class of slow-witted village children who had only lately learned to read when he could have been giving lectures to advanced students and learned societies.

By this time any official doubts about the school had been removed and, much to Henslow's satisfaction, was recommended for the training of pupil teachers. An Inspector who had examined the school felt called on to correct local criticisms that the religious instruction in the school was being neglected. It was 'quite equal to any imparted to poor children in parish schools in general.' He also added: 'I had no reason to think that the botanical lessons interfered with the due study of the usual subjects of a National School.'

As Henslow survived one criticism, another would be invented. It was only after many years of persistent effort and stubborn deafness to local opinion that a truce was reached, due partly to the undoubted high regard of his work there held by the educational world outside and partly to the huge success of the Professor's botanical expeditions in which, eventually, every one in the village joined.

Nothing like these excursions had ever been known before. They entailed travelling in a train and usually to the seaside, a double helping of excitement almost too much for some who had never before left their village. There were some, indeed, who declared a fear of travelling so fast or of seeing such a vast amount of water. When the train entered the tunnel at Ipswich there were shouts and whistles of excited panic. The open-mouthed wonder of going down the Orwell by river steamer to Harwich and on another occasion of being shown over the impressive Landguard Fort by the military were treats to remember. As always, the Professor sandwiched these lighter tit-bits between the bread of serious and painstaking botanical observation. It was always in his mind not merely to indicate the wonders of nature but to encourage an investigating curiosity in his pupils.

So popular did these excursions become that something like 200 villagers would turn out in their Sunday best to take part and because of Henslow's meticulous preparations the Hitcham contingent achieved a reputation for their lively interest and good behaviour. The most successful of all the expeditions and a peak of achievement for the Professor himself was that on which no fewer than 283 people, including farmers, local gentry and dissenting clergymen forgot their differences and travelled with the village rustics in a solid body to Cambridge. Here, Henslow was able to link the work of the school botany class with the advanced experiments he had made at the University and extended the wonder of his rural company by visits to museums and collections there.

Here, too, he was able to provide more than the customary tit-bits of entertainment for the group, for when feet began to drag and tongues to feel dry, he called a halt at the doors of Downing Hall. As if the immediate surroundings were not awe-inspiring enough, no less a person than the Vice Chancellor himself stood there to welcome them all. Ushered into the great hall, nearly 300 Hitcham wanderers sat down together to take good helpings of plum pudding and beer, until all became mellowed in good-natured fellowship.

For the rustics it was the day of a lifetime. As for the farmers who had once opposed every effort of the Professor to bring botany into the village school, so impressed were they with the success of the outing that they soon after presented him with a silver cup. It was a generous but unnecessary gift for Professor Henslow. His satisfaction and reward came from a different source — the life and interest he now saw in village faces in contrast to the former surliness. They could never again completely lose hope.

Alice Driver — Martyr

The idea that wisdom can exist without a grounding of education may have very little credence among savants. In the general concensus it is knowledge that is power. To suggest that knowledge of the world as it is does not necessarily contribute to long-term thought, is no doubt irreverent, even if true. The intelligent, educated individual knows the world in impressive detail. It is a machine of which he can name all the parts, all the functions. It would need an idiot with his own natural wisdom to ask why the machine functions so, why it cannot be replaced by a completely different set of concepts which may not be a machine at all.

To such nonsensical questions the eyes of the educated machine-minder will glaze over with contempt. He knows what there is to know, the world is an open book. There is no point in making suppositious remarks about a machine that functions very well, thank you. Facts, after all, are facts.

Indeed they are, and not ideas. At the risk of being seen as completely beyond the pale by the intelligentsia one could add, given courage enough, that facts can easily tend to get in the way of more distant views and prove a barrier to simple moral conviction. Wisdom without knowledge is by no means a contradiction if we are to accept the value of the contribution that some unlettered people have made to the world. Thinking of such people makes me wonder, as a countryman, whether a close communion with nature does not make a worthwhile replacement for education in some cases. There was the girl from Grundisburgh, near Woodbridge, for example — long ago in the days of religious persecution. Like that other Suffolk girl, Margaret Catchpole and like that classic voice of natural wisdom, Joan of Arc, she worked hard and alone in the fields during her formative years. There was scarcely a ha'porth of education

between the three of them, yet each succeeded in asto-
nishing the world of learning and in particular the judges at
their separate trials for the paltry misdemeanours for which
they were convicted. It could be pointed out, no doubt, that
it was education and the law that prevailed and punished the
women but this was an empty triumph by modern lights.

Of this formidable trio of village maidens, the least
known, by reason of the long lapse of time, is Alice Driver,
daughter of a ploughman (as was Margaret Catchpole) of
Grundisburgh. This comely girl worked in the open air from
her earliest days, teaching her small hands to grip and
wrench the handles of the plough and her small shoulders to
carry the yoke for the pails of milk, since this was the
labouring life to which she was destined. When in due course
a neighbouring farm labourer came to court her she
accepted this, too, with peasant equanimity. Married, she
continued to work on the land and, for all anyone knows,
lived contentedly enough with her husband. Scarcely anything is known about the man. Only by default can his
character be assessed for it is clear that, though he was
doubtless adequate to deal with the daily grind of their
humble lives, when greater qualities were required he
remained earth-bound and blunt-witted. He was not in
evidence, therefore, as being in support of his wife at any
stage of her long and agonising journey to her death at the
stake.

Perhaps the first murmur of future trouble in Alice's
settled life was when her father came to the field where she
was working and told her that the young King Edward VI
had died. There was fear that the few years' peace they had
known would come to a bloody end should Mary Tudor take
the throne. Like most village folk, Alice would find it hard
to be disloyal to the Protestant teachings of her youth and
she would be dismayed at the ease with which more
sophisticated people were already changing to the Catholic
faith. Suddenly, friends were no longer friends and spies
were suspected everywhere, even in this remote village. The
heavy hand of Mary Tudor reached into every cottage to

demand that the family committed itself to participation in the new forms of worship. In the farmhouse home of Alice Driver the requirement aroused the sturdy East Anglian trait of independence at all costs. She would form her own opinion, thank you, and for true guidance would rely on the direct counsel of the Bible, which she had taught herself to read. For some time she continued to attend the local church regularly, as did all the villagers but after the new rituals were introduced she confided to someone that she thought the proceedings 'idolatrous'. When the minister heard the comment and noted also that Alice was falling away from her attendance to take the Sacrament, he passed her name on to those authorities interested in the punishment of backsliders.

Perhaps the matter in itself would have been of no great danger to her but for another happening that occurred at the same time and which forced her, through common humanity, to show kindness to a hunted victim of the purge. A young weaver named Alexander Gooch, who lived in nearby Woodbridge, had been rash enough to speak out against the Pope as the head of the Church and now was in fear for his life. The notorious Justice Noone heard of the fact and promised that the young recalcitrant would suffer the full consequences, when caught. Such minor hindrances as this to the cause gave Noone the utmost pleasure to deal with, since he was able to add to the general Catholic persecution his own personal, dedicated cruelty.

In the meantime, Gooch had fled from his home and hidden for some days in the countryside about, living as well as he could. In the end, when almost exhausted, he came surreptitiously to the door of the farm girl Alice Driver, who in pity took him in. The act was one of instinctive sympathy and had little to do with religion but it placed the girl at once in danger of the direst punishment. As the mob of searchers led by Justice Noone himself reached the village of Grundis-burgh the villagers turned out to watch and no doubt there was more than one spiteful finger ready to point the way to the Driver's home.

Inside the farmhouse, the tired young weaver told Alice of the hue and cry that followed close behind and the couple tried desperately to think of a way of escape. Already they could hear the shouts of the pursuers, above all the harsh commands of Justice Noone as he ordered the search from his perch astride his great black horse. A few minutes more and they would be at the farm and turning out every corner and hiding place.

Alice threw a shawl about her and drew the young man out through the back door in desperate haste and would have run madly by the footpath through the fields to out-distance the pursuers but that Alexander was weak with hunger and tired from long exposure to the weather. With all her young arm's strength she helped and urged him along but it was no use. Soon they would be seen and overtaken. In despair for her as much as for himself, he tried to persuade her to leave him and return to her home where she would be safe from implication, but Alice calmly refused. There was no doubt in her mind that, whatever religion said about it, it was the right thing to help an unfortunate fellow creature.

Among the outbuildings of the farm where they now stood, was a small stack of hay placed handy for the feeding of horses. In a desperate effort to hide, the two burrowed into the heap, covered themselves as best they could and waited anxiously as the sound of the chase grew nearer. Within a few minutes there were horses and followers all about the farm with Justice Noone pointing out all the likely hiding places. It was an inspired cruelty on the part of some group of village oafs to fetch pitch-forks from the barn and with the long bare spikes investigate the stack of hay. Both Alice and Alexander were badly wounded and could not resist calling out in pain, much to the delight of their persecutors. Justice Noone surveyed the couple in triumph as they emerged from their hiding place and had them put at once in a cart to be driven to the gaol at Melton.

It was from this point on that Alice somehow assumed a new stature in pride and courage that would probably have amazed her husband and her farm-labouring acquaintances. Under the guise of the simple peasant girl she had kept subdued the spirit that now shone out in anger at the injustice that she found all around her. Fear no longer oppressed her — she was already free of it. There was comfort, too, in knowing that there were many who wept within the privacy of their own homes to see her taken away to languish at Melton for no crime but that which her accusers had invented.

When the time came for the trial, the two were taken to the Assizes at Bury St. Edmunds where Alice at once showed the character that was to be an inspiration to others but inevitably caused her own undoing. After all, she was but a country girl, using the familiar voice and idiom of rural Suffolk and had she shown a proper humility before her betters, expressing contrition for her wrongs and offering a full recantation of her faith, she might have survived. As it was, her steadfast honesty and disregard for her personal situation incensed the judges whose sense of justice had already been lost in the demands of the Catholic purge. As if she welcomed the encounter with the chief interrogator, Sir Clement Higham, she smiled often as she parried his loaded questions, though well aware that whatever answers she gave they would gain her very little mercy. Already she had sealed her own fate by refusing to take note of the Queen's name with sufficient reverence. Later she was asked to give an opinion of the Queen and she answered that the most likely comparison was that of Jezebel. As court officials gasped in disbelief, Sir Clement Higham jumped to his feet, pointed at the girl with shaking finger and ordered that her ears be cut off.

'Thank you, sir,' was Alice's response. 'If that is what you need to satisfy your idolatrous beliefs, you shall have my ears. But there are others with ears and eyes and senses and steady hearts, too, who will stand against you in the end.'

The mutilation was carried out immediately. Lying in the gaol at Melton, waiting for the trial to continue and nursing her several wounds, Alice braced herself for the ordeal to come with such success that, on going into the court-room again, she managed to smile at all who were gathered there. Dr. Spencer, Chancellor of Norwich, asked her bitterly if she were laughing at the judges and she answered blithely: 'If you choose to think so, sir.'

The proceedings of the trial were soon lost in a rigmarole of dogma and religious discourse through which Alice's simple replies sometimes shone out like a light.

'What sort of scriptures have you read?' asked Dr. Spencer scornfully, apparently intending to exhibit Alice as an illiterate plough-girl.

'Why, God's book,' she answered.

'Well, what kind of book is it you call God's book?'

'Why, the Bible. What would you call it?'

At one point, as she hesitated to answer a question, she was prompted by a priest standing nearby to answer the judges' questions quickly.

'Well, priest,' she said. 'I came here not to talk to you but with your master but if you want me to talk to you, then you must tell your master to be quiet.' The priest said no other word during the rest of the trial.

Those observers who quietly sympathised with Alice were distraught at her very courage, knowing that the judges would take it ill to be embarrassed by some peasant girl. Only Alice herself seemed to be untouched by it all and those who watched felt that, though she was likely to lose all, she had gained something too. In a way, they had all gained something. With pride in their sorrow they heard the summing up. Then Alexander Gooch was brought in to stand beside Alice while Sir Clement Higham ordered that they should be burned alive together at the stake on the Cornhill, Ipswich.

For whatever sins she had committed — and they were little enough to modern eyes, Alice lost her life at the age of 30 at the behest of religious bigots. At the very end there was some small reward for her courage for when the populace gathered on the Cornhill there were cheers and shouts of sympathy. As Alice and the weaver stood chained to their stakes above the heap of faggots before the fire was lit, many people rushed forward to hold her hand and bless her. From the gallery of the Shambles where the notables of Ipswich could sit and watch the entertainment in comfort, the Sheriff shouted to his men to arrest those who had shown sympathy for the prisoners. Immediately there was a great surge forward of the crowd in order to thwart the efforts of the officers and obscure the identity of people in the throng. For some minutes the crowd encircled the pyre, touching the hands of the two condemned, some kneeling to pray. There was a great silence then on the Cornhill from the moment that the faggots were ignited to the dying of the last guttering flame.

Richard Cobbold — Scribe

Unwilling though the Rev. Richard Cobbold undoubtedly was to take up the living of Wortham near Diss, when proffered by the bishop, it must be a matter of immense satisfaction to all people interested in the village life of the past that he did so. During the years that he spent there — something near half a century in all — he amassed a great treasury of notes and sketches, cameos and paintings, all concerning the people, the farms and the houses nearby and all done with a subtlety and shrewdness that would escape all but the most dedicated observer. As if not satisfied that he had described his subjects adequately in words, he accompanied each literary cameo with a lovingly executed sketch — all the more telling for their lack of proportion and finish. All in all, Richard Cobbold's gallery of subjects form a fascinating insight into life about the village green in the nineteenth century. Whether they come from farmhouse, hall or hovel, they all receive the same close and astute attention. His curiosity as to his fellow villagers was insatiable.

This Richard Cobbold was, of course, the author of *Margaret Catchpole, Freston Tower* and several other books. Though belonging to the wealthy and influential brewing family of Cliff Quay, Ipswich, he occupied a fairly insignificant place in it, being the twentieth and penultimate of all the children from two marriages. At the tail-end of the family it seemed appropriate, perhaps to leave to others the concerns of business and go into the Church as he did, simultaneously with his younger brother Edward. There followed a curacy in Ipswich where, under the aegis of his formidable mother, he indulged with complete content in parochial affairs and in writing. It came as an intrusion upon his settled life then to be offered a living so remote as that of Wortham.

It was, no doubt, a much more out-of-the-way place than it seems now. Travel was slow, the country roads in atrocious condition and it must have seemed a kind of exile at first to the young parson. Not only was he to leave the bosom of a large and important urban family for the undoubted boredom of a half-forgotten hamlet but in particular he was forced to sever the strong apron strings of his mother, who was ever the most loved and admired person in his life. However, there was no alternative. The Bishop was insistent and the break had to come. In 1827, Cobbold built his own rectory at Wortham and occupied it in the following year. Immediately, it seems, the bucolic contrasts of rural life seized his imagination. Out came the note-book and sketch-pad that were to be the constant accompaniments to his ministry and all the oddities of his faithful flock were thence-forward fully recorded. His early resentment was soon forgotten and as year followed year he found his own life knitting more and more closely into the lives of the villagers. Only long acquaintance and a shrewd judgment could have allowed him to sum up the local characters as he did.

There was Noah Fake, for instance: 'Noah Fake, the village carpenter, the village politician, the village factotum, performing almost all offices — and knowing himself to be but a poor performer. Poor man, who might have been a rich man had he but done well with what he had.

'He came to me ten years ago, with tears in his eyes, saying: "Sir, I feel that I'm a goin'. Yes sir, I feel that I'm a goin'. I have not long to live — and yet I should not like to be forgotten. I hope, sir, you will make a sketch of me. I should not like old Noah to be forgotten."

'He has a long head and a strong head, can see far and is yet short-sighted. Wishes to be right and yet does wrong. How strange are the characters of men and this man is one of them. He will read all day, keep his Sabbaths exact, talk most deeply and seriously of his convictions and in another moment set them all aside and give way to temptation. Anyone would pronounce him wise who knew him not.'

And what was Cobbold's opinion of old Thomas God-
dard? 'He was a vivacious, merry old man . . . so punctual to
his work as a labourer that his master never knew him to be
late any one morning when he went to work — nor a minute
too early when he left off.

'Though he died in a miserable hovel — in fact in an
outshed which he shared with one William Rose — to the
hour of his death he always said: "I love the sight of the Ling
on which I have cut turf from my boyhood and would rather
give up the ghost there than be a tenant of the Union House
in my old days".'

One can imagine old Thomas expressing these sentiments
while the parson, sketch-book before him, had him seated
comfortably in the sun for his face and person to be tolerably
copied and put away for the judgment of posterity. Thomas
was then 82 but hale and hearty and he was able to enjoy the
sight of the Ling for another eight years.

Cobbold was ever tolerant of the black sheep. His word-
picture of the wrong-doer George Minter shows more
sympathy than condemnation. 'He is without doubt the
scamp of the country. He has been sent to gaol twelve times
for refusing to work and vagabondism and yet no reforma-
tion takes place in the man. I think the man is mad. At least
he has got into such irrational yet harmless habits and has so
completely driven himself from the society of his fellow-men
that he can scarcely be called sane.

'He speaks in the pompous language of the theatre.
"Yonder is my mansion, sir," pointing to the barn. "And
there, let me tell you, I sleep as soundly on my bed of straw
as you do on your bed of down. I envy neither king nor
queen, lord nor lady, priest nor squire. I do no harm to
anyone. I take what is given to me and I would not thank
anyone for more than my daily bread. I am a philosopher.
My philosophy is this: Be content. I never was otherwise."

'Now there is much philosophy in the speech — yet all his
friends are ashamed of him. One gives him a herring,
another a penny, another a crust of bread. If sent to the
treadmill, he always comes out with a character for

44

quietness, but the moment he is out he becomes again a solitary man. It is said he was crossed in love!'

It must be remembered that Richard Cobbold was not only the spiritual head of the village but a writer of considerable literary invention and he may have rounded off his characters sometimes with a touch of idealism. However, the ring of truth is always there even when he describes the funnier sides of village life. How he must have chuckled at the Fuller couple and the way they led their lives!

'James Fuller, a fine old labourer, was very highly respected by every master who employed him. He was one of the kindest and best of husbands to a wife who was confined to her bed sixteen years. James was a practically pious old man, paid the most deferential respect to his wife who was wonderfully learned, so James said. James was a good old man: he has a fine head and altogether benign expression of countenance. He died when aged 89.

'Judy Fuller was in her younger days so completely overcome by nervous disorganisation that from the age of 25 until she died at the advanced age of 85 she always used to say to her daughters: "Ah, my dears, I shall not live another twelvemonth."

'She was a living instance of giving way to inactivity before her proper time and like many who find it pleasant to be waited on, she took to her bed and stayed there for sixteen years. She was always contented and rejoiced to converse with persons of superior education. Her cottage and the bed in which she spent so many years of her life, were as remarkable as herself. James had purchased the state bed at the auction at the Hall. It was blue cloth and silver ornaments, a coat of arms being worked at the head. But the cottage! Festoons of cobwebs hung like icicles from the black rafters. Nor would Judy permit the spiders to be killed. She literally enjoyed their society. She was as honest as she was pious and would not take even a sixpence donation of the wealthy when she did not actually want it.'

In time, Richard Cobbold became the complete country cleric, fishing and hunting to serve his own amusement, following the accepted tenets of his religion and showing a pastoral care that earned him respect and admiration. In his study at the Rectory, he continued to write in beautiful longhand with scarcely a single correction all the details of Wortham life, its farms and large houses, its cottages and hovels, its craftsmen and labourers and was as much concerned with the humblest member of the community as with the most important. He grieved over the poor shoesmith, Robert Potter:

'He works more hours and faster than any man in the parish of Wortham. No man works harder than this neat, upright man. Yet very few are worse paid for all their labours than he. He has to make and mend soles and trust people until he can obtain any payment for his work. If the village cobbler could be paid by the labourers of the parish he would be well off. But so many poor people have to pay at a shilling a time that he scarcely gets enough to support himself.'

At the gardener's house there was drama of a high order: 'Here lived and died Jas. Flatman, gardener at the Hall. He and all his family lay ill with typhus fever and no one could be found to nurse them. Rewards were offered but so malignant was the fever that the man and four children died before anyone could be found to attend to them. When Mrs. Gillam heard of it she said "If my husband will let me go, I will brave the danger." She did go and saved the life of the woman and four of the children. Yet she neither sought nor asked for any reward. We speak of courage! What is greater courage than to go and sleep in a room with dead and dying people with malignant typhus fever? Have you ever done such a thing? Flora Nightingale was a good nurse but did she ever do such a thing? Never! Nor did I.'

An old man for whom Cobbold had a special respect was Soldier Smith. 'He served in the Peninsular Wars and was a Waterloo man. He was an old pensioner but a very active man. He could not do farming work, but used to work in his allotment and earn a penny by cutting turf for the winter. His death was remarkable in affording an instance of the quick departure out of this life and of the sagacity of a dog. Old Richard was often seen to seat himself in his own home-made wheel-barrow to rest himself. One day he sat down and never rose up again — but as he sat so he remained. A passing pedlar's dog observed something in the old man which several who passed him did not observe. The dog went up to him, barked at him, smelt of him and lay down at his feet. His master's whistle could not induce him to stir. The dog's conduct moved the attention of two labourers who were turning over a muck-heap on the verge of the common. They came up to the old man and then the dog immediately ran after his master. They found Richard Smith quite dead and seated as easy as if he were asleep.'

The dog's action much impressed the Rector, who in due course recorded some other remarkable creatures at Wortham. There were the geese of Mary Ann Harbour, for example, who claimed that they needed more looking after, more scolding and sometimes more thwacking than any obstinate child. Cobbold comments: 'It was quite ridiculous to see how "Go you on to your nest!" would set the creature back on her eggs as quickly as possible.'

It was to the Rector's constant sorrow that so many of the village characters were given to drinking at the public house. The carpenter, the mole-catcher and the blacksmith were among those given black marks on this account. Cobbold believed, indeed, that the blacksmith's shop had been built deliberately by the landlady of the Queen's Head close beside the pub so that the idlers and gossipers could move between forge and bar with very little effort. There was also the near-fatal affair of John Bush when he arrived home somewhat fuddled with drink. To recover himself before entering the house he sat on the edge of the well in the yard and promptly fell in. He fell sixty feet into six feet of water and must have come to an end there had not his daughter heard the rattle of the chain and woken her husband in time to rescue the old man.

Inevitably, most of Richard Cobbold's contacts with his parishioners were at times of trouble and distress, but he happily records one occasion when he received a tiny but welcome acknowledgment of the gratitude and affection in which he was held.

'I must narrate here an incident of a dear child who loved me, and gave me the only proof of her love that she could give me — a genuine kiss! Stare, ye philosophers! Ye cold and distant monarchs of propriety! Stare at the simplicity of a child, who could not help giving it me though unsolicited, unexpected and totally unaccountable for at the time. I stood at my iron gate, holding it open for the children who were leaving the Sunday School. One little girl of the name of Woods, after going a little way on the road, returned and to my astonishment, with tears in her eyes, put up her little face to kiss me. I let her do so and she ran after her companions smiling in her tears.

'Next day I saw her mother and told her of the incident. "She told me of it herself, sir. She thought that as she is going to London tomorrow she might never see you again. So that is why she ran back and gave you a kiss." '

This extraordinary gallery of absorbing portraits by Richard Cobbold overlooks no one. There is no one in the village below his notice: all are revealed here and their secrets known. Without his deep interest in their lives these simple folk would have passed out of knowledge with no more substance than of fleeting shadows. As it is, he holds them there for us for ever.

Rowland Lance — Knight

The eccentricity of Mr. Rowland Lance was short-lived but spectacular. It burst forth the more intensely when at last released from Mr. Lance's hitherto respectable life-style and it struck the few people destined to be witnesses quite dumb with wonder. It happened one summer some half-way through the eighteenth century when George the Second was on the throne and it rated for a time with the recent news of Prince Charlie's march south to Derby. Unfortunately, it was a type of lunacy that could not be indulged in privately and in public it very quickly raised such a degree of intolerance that caused it, regretfully, to be abandoned.

Before this untimely event, Mr. Lance was regarded as a paragon of rectitude in the small West Suffolk village where he lived, a man conscious of his good fortune in being born on the right side of the gulf between rich and poor and one who was a scholar of some achievement. His house was substantial and well-staffed with four servants. There was a carriage and horses at his disposal and all the contemporary requirements of a well-off bachelor. Most prized of his possessions was a considerable library of books for he was a voracious reader, particularly of tales of the past that told of deeds of valour and chivalry and the adventures of gallant knights. Sometimes he would be so carried away in the reading of Mallory's *Morte d'Arthur* that he would recite some of the lines aloud:

'Sir Launcelot, thou wert the courteoust knight that ever bare shield; and thou wert the truest friend that every bestrad a horse; and thou wert the meekest man and the gentlest that ever ate in hall with ladies; and thou wert the sternest knight to thy mortal foe that ever put spear in the rest.'

Beyond this mild idiosyncrasy, there was nothing in Mr. Rowland Lance's behaviour to suggest the transformation about to take place and the domestic routine continued in well-ordered fashion until June. Then, suddenly and completely, he disappeared. The servants became curious, then concerned, relatives were sent for and concern became anxiety. All possible ideas were checked and advertisements begging for news of his whereabouts placed in newspapers and on hoardings. In the end it had to be admitted that there was not the slightest clue or shred of help from any quarter. It had to be assumed that Lance was dead or at least did not intend to come back to continue his former life. The house and all his possessions were sold, the servants soon dispersed to other employers. All that was left was the memory of a tolerant, gentle scholar.

In fact, Mr. Rowland Lance was far from being dead. He was living in modest but adequate style no more than fifty miles away in rural Essex. In a fairly remote village there the most prominent establishment was the Prince's Arms, owned and managed by a retired Excise man named Foster. By some concordance of interests revealed in earlier visits, Foster and Lance had reached a friendship of sorts within the mutual recognition of Lance's much higher social position. Though not a complete sycophant, Foster had the admiration of a humble and aspiring man for the obvious scholarship and humanity of his visitor and in general was ready to agree to anything that Lance suggested.

Lance's arrival that summer morning with scarcely any possessions save a few books on ancient chivalry and an adequate purse aroused Foster's best instincts as a host, stifling his immediate curiosity and putting his best room at the other's disposal. For the next few days Lance wandered about in the neighbourhood or sat and read under the trees in the orchard and generally behaved in a rather abstracted manner. Not knowing anything of the immense commotion being raised by his guest's disappearance from home, the inn-keeper inquired no further into the reasons for his protracted stay. He was glad to sit with him sometimes and listen to the tales of King Arthur and the Knights of the Round Table. When Lance mentioned to him that he would dearly like to acquire a suit of armour such as knights once wore, his host found himself agreeing to seek around for such a thing.

Armour alone, considered Lance to himself, was not enough. His horse would need the trappings appropriate to the steed of a medieval knight and there would have to be a squire, beyond doubt, to ride beside the knight — for whoever heard of a knight without a squire? He pledged his host to obtain secretly all the equipment needed for a campaign into distant parts and this was faithfully agreed to. It was no surprise to Foster to discover, after inquiries far and near, that it was practically impossible to obtain a suit of armour. At the end of a week's searching he had acquired only a few remnants of ancient arms. These were a helmet that had once belonged to a soldier of the Light Horse, a shield of formidable size carrying the arms of some Scottish chieftain, a pair of horse pistols without any ammunition and a sword.

As for the horse, it was not difficult to provide a suitable mount but in the absence of genuine knightly accoutrements it was decided to embellish it with pennants and coloured cloths. A squire was eventually recruited with some bribery in the person of Norris Lambert, a grocer's assistant, who was also clothed and mounted in as valiant a manner as possible. From first to last Lambert lacked the fine spirit of crusading adventure that inspired his master and saw the exercise only as a relief from the boredom of weighing bags of sugar. What he was required to do he had only the vaguest idea except that he must keep company with his master at all times. Since he had never before mounted a horse, it was some days of sore discomfort before he was judged ready for duty.

All this time the innkeeper had assisted in the preparations without feeling a need to interfere but with a growing concern as to the outcome. Questions that he sometimes asked of Lance about returning to his former life, about his house, servants and relatives, received only the vaguest of answers. Lance seemed to be more and more absorbed in thoughts of a prospective expedition in full knightly attire

51

and due ceremony, not, as Foster realised, because of mere exhibitionism but because he genuinely believed that a return to the ways of chivalry and honour was the only way to counteract the base manners and boorish attitudes of the time. He intended that he and his squire would ride across the country to the far west where the knights of old had performed their deeds of valour on behalf of the oppressed and try to continue there the traditions begun so long ago.

Lambert, the grocer's boy, joined in the preparations with as much interest as generous wages could buy and spent much of his time at the Prince's Arms in trying to find a quiet refuge from his master's enthusiasms. The clothes that had been found up for him, supposedly similar to those once worn by a squire in attendance on his lord seemed to him to be ridiculous enough. Sitting in such clothes on the back of an under-sized horse within sight of grinning ostlers gave him even less pleasure. Also, he could tell, there would be worse to come. He was not at all surprised when told that before the expedition began it was necessary to follow the knightly custom of keeping vigil over the arms. It seemed to Lambert to show an excess of reverence for a pair of antiquated pistols and a sword with a broken scabbard but he duly supported his master in the long night watch.

By next morning and the end of the vigil, further ideas had come into the mind of the would-be crusading knight. In fact, as he pointed out, he was not really a knight at all. It was something that had to be rectified before they set out. Once more the innkeeper was drawn into the affair. As a former Exciseman and therefore a devoted servant of the King, Mr. Lance assured him, it was logical to assume that he derived certain powers from such an exalted position and could be expected to perform the service of conferring a knighthood since the King himself could not be present.

Accordingly, the sword was brought into ceremonial use and Mr. Rowland Lance arose from his knees as the undoubted knight, Sir Orlando. A tired Lambert heard with complete resignation that henceforward he would be called Lamberto. During the next few hours the couple were able to rest and refresh themselves before the crusade began. Then the knight donned his full armour and accoutrements, bade the lagging squire to follow close behind and set off, to the wonder of inn lackeys and lookers-on.

The road westwards led inevitably towards London and as they approached the metropolis the two adventurers could not but notice the increase in the traffic as well as of ridicule from certain groups of people, whether mounted or on foot. Such insolence was exceedingly tiresome to Sir Orlando, who flashed about with his sword occasionally to indicate that he would have no nonsense from ill-bred rustics. It was even more tiresome to Lamberto who hung back from the knight like one who would have liked to find himself transformed again into a grocer's boy weighing up endless bags of sugar.

Various small carts had overtaken the couple as they rode along. Now, suddenly, a very noisy conveyance began to come up from behind. It was a closed waggon with three carters attending and from inside there came the deafening shrieks and squeals of a load of pigs being taken to the market. Sir Orlando seemed to take an instant dislike to the three ruffians on the waggon whom he took to be devils running off with wailing human souls. It was clear to him that the whole thing was due to enchantment. Action was called for.

In an instant he had drawn his sword and advanced with a challenging yell just as the cart drew level. The doughty squire, surprised into sudden action, came up too in support just in time to be knocked off his horse by the lunging draft horse, set in a wild panic by the appearance of the attacking knight. At once they were off at a gallop, dragging the cart at a breakneck speed and almost unseating the three unsavoury gentlemen who alternately sawed at the reins and shook their fists toward the diminishing figure of the crusader. Lamberto was still on the ground complaining bitterly and the knight helped him to rise. He was bruised and shaken and it took a good deal of persuasion to get him back again on his horse.

Sir Orlando was not in the least put out by the incident. 'For our first attempt to combat evil forces, it was not a bad achievement,' he decided. 'Next time we shall surely succeed in halting such an equipage — for there is no doubt from the unearthly noises that it was enchanted.'

'Some achievement,' groaned Lamberto. 'It may appear to be an achievement to you but it gives me no satisfaction to ride a horse with all these bruises. Anyway, when it comes down to reality, all that we were attacking was a load of shrieking pigs.'

'How stupid can you be?' exclaimed the knight. 'That is all part of the enchantment. Fortunately, I think we have intervened in time to break the spell.'

In the meantime the waggon full of pigs had reached its destination at a cattle market where the animals were unloaded. The irate carters could scarcely contain themselves in their haste to set off on the return journey to avenge themselves on the madman who had attacked them with a sword. It was not long before they came to where the knight and squire were making their rather slow progress along the roadside. The sight of the two riders in their fantastic dress and trappings seemed to enrage the men still further and they at once jumped down from the waggon intent on doing battle. Seeing that he was being attacked by giants, Sir Orlando immediately drew his sword, calling on his reluctant squire to give aid. The sword proved to be not a very effective weapon when put to the test and the attackers soon robbed him of it. Sir Orlando then produced his horse pistols which seemed to gain much more respect. The knight had never regarded the pistols very seriously since they were not appropriate arms for a man of chivalry and they had never been used or even loaded. However, they had a fearsome enough appearance to keep the giants at bay until one of them picked up a formidable-sized stone and aimed it at the knight, knocking him off his horse.

What happened after that was beyond his knowing. He lay unconscious for what must have been quite a long time because when he came to he was quite alone. The waggon had gone and the belligerent carters with it, so had Lamberto, so had his own horse. There was nothing but the dry ditch into which he had fallen and a splitting headache to remind him of the short and not entirely victorious battle with the giants. He spent some few minutes re-assembling his ideas and feeling very unwell. Eventually he spied his horse quietly grazing some way off and when he managed to heave his aching body into the saddle it was not forward to the crusades that he turned but back again in the direction he had come. There was no going on at the present time. His squire had deserted him or had been taken prisoner by the giants — he himself was wounded in body and spirit. He must return to his base and then re-organise the expedition. It could well be that he would have to set off on a rescue mission to some castle where Lamberto was being held by the giants.

On the same day that he had started out with such high hopes of liberating the oppressed, Sir Orlando returned to the Prince's Arms. He had been beaten in the lists, he confided to the innkeeper. He would have to spend some days in meditation.

It was during the period of meditation, which kept the knight very subdued for a time, that the doughty squire returned, looking even more woe-begone than before. His story was far removed from the fantasy of giants and evil enchantments. Nor, he assured the knight who gave him a very warm welcome, had he been kept a prisoner in a castle by a witch. The plain facts were that after the battle with the waggoners, Lamberto had been arrested for being concerned with an affray and disturbing the King's peace, had been taken to London and lodged in a cell until called to appear before a magistrate. The magistrate had shown very little sympathy for the cause of knightly deeds and was obviously somewhat perplexed at Lamberto's odd manner of dress but eventually accepted that he was merely the tool of another, and bigger, idiot and sent him away.

The journey home was one that Lamberto would long remember, pursued by missiles, taunts and laughter, as well

as by every urchin from miles around. As soon as he
returned to the inn, he lost no time in discarding the apparel
of a squire and the name of Lamberto. His words of farewell
directed to Sir Orlando were neither curtly nor chivalrous.

So ended the strange delusion of Mr. Rowland Lance, two
hundreds years after Cervantes had sent his own crusading
pair off on their adventures. Had he known the story,
perhaps Norris Lambert might have echoed the words of
Sancho Panza about his own master:

'He is a muddle-headed fool, but with occasional lucid
intervals.'

Abraham Cawston —
Heir to Millions

Some say that it is good fortune to be born in East Anglia and a blessed lot to be able to live out one's life here within reach of the fresh breezes from the sea. Fortunate it may well be, remembering the adage that health and long life comes before all other benefits, but it has not always seemed the most propitious part of the country for those more interested in financial rewards. Perhaps they were mistaken in this, for there are those who have made fortunes here — and lost them too, no doubt — among whom was the Cambridgeshire lad so abundantly showered with unexpected wealth it seemed that he was chosen by the gods.

The story of Abraham Westerman Cawston comes from one or two newspaper articles and other incidental material of the time, which establish the basic facts of this incredible inheritance and of the admirable young man who received it. By tradition it is those who are rich who are entitled to be eccentric and in this Arabian Nights tale both the main participants could be judged eligible by that criterion. The wealth concerned was so immense, the circumstances so unusual that the countryside was at first incredulous then caught up in the wonder of a fairy-tale come true, until society, parliament and the Lord Chancellor himself were in some degree involved.

Abraham Cawston was born at Chippenham, near Newmarket, in 1800, the youngest son of a hard-working small farmer. His insignificant place in a large family did not obscure for a moment his exceptional promise. From the earliest years he was not only quick and eager to learn but was supported by a modest, courteous attitude that endeared him to everyone. Older brothers destined to work on the family farm showed no envy when the local

57

clergyman undertook to educate the boy and it was on his earnest recommendation that Abraham was later sent as a boarder to an eminent school at Shrewsbury. He was then fourteen and he attended at Shrewsbury for the next three years — until, in fact, the extraordinary events of the inheritance. During those years the boy's father, John Cawston, saw the rewards of the family's sacrifices in sending him to such a distinguished place of learning for all the reports were of an intelligent and diligent pupil, as popular as he was clever and one likely to fulfil his promise to the utmost in some important career.

When Abraham reached his seventeenth year, the Headmaster himself, the Rev. Dr. Butler, wrote to John Cawston in terms of unstinted admiration for the boy's good work and influence in the school and expressed the hope that he would in due course enter the Church. It was such a letter as to bring great satisfaction to John Cawston and his wife. Only one small point puzzled them for at the end of the letter the Doctor had added the observation that Abraham seemed to have a great deal of pocket money. It was not a good thing, he thought, either for Abraham or for the rest of the boys and he advised the parents to reduce the amount. John Cawston must have scratched his head at this, for he gave his son only the slimmest allowance and it seemed that there was a misunderstanding somewhere. It was a small matter, after all, when put beside all the good reports.

As John worked on the farm, however, the puzzle of the excessive pocket money returned frequently to his mind and he decided that he must remember to take Abraham to task about it. When the boy came home for the summer holidays there was the harvest about to begin and more important matters to think about so that the matter only came to be mentioned casually later on. Abraham had been listening with modest pleasure to his father's praise for his school reports when John remembered the pocket money. When he asked the boy for an explanation, the inquiry seemed to affect him considerably. He remained quiet for a time as if trying to think of the right answer, then took on a serious air and asked his father if he would wait for a time before he gave him an explanation. There were good reasons why he was asking this, he asserted, as his father would soon learn, but he was unable to reveal at that moment his position in the matter.

Astonished and rather troubled by this, John Cawston felt that he must insist upon having more information. At this, the boy gave in reluctantly but with his usual good manners and promised to tell his father the whole story but asked that he would keep it secret for a time until he could produce more evidence as to the truth of it. It was a strange story he had to tell and so much outside ordinary experience that it could be difficult to believe. Abraham then straight away told his father the full account of what had happened and why their lives would never be the same again.

Two terms before, on returning to school at Shrewsbury from his home, he had followed the usual routine of catching the stage coach at the Sun Hotel in Cambridge. He had shared the inside of the coach during the long journey with a gentleman of considerable age, white-haired and frail, a man who spoke good English but with a foreign accent. Soon, a conversation began, polite at first but as different matters were discussed opinions between the two differed widely and tempers rose. It seemed to Abraham that the stranger was fixed in his views and was too old to yield to new ideas. By the time that the two passengers reached Shrewsbury, where they both got down, their mutual disagreement led them to part with scarcely a civil word.

So far as Abraham was concerned, that was the end of the matter. He was astonished when, about two weeks later, a groom appeared at the school, mounted on one horse and leading another, with a letter requesting that Abraham would accompany the groom to the home of his master, Don Gaspar de Quintilla. The invitation was couched in the most friendly terms and was revealed as coming from Abraham's aged companion on the coach. He learned too, as he rode with the groom to keep the appointment, that his host was an extremely rich and powerful man who lived in a mansion just outside Shrewsbury.

It was the beginning of the great adventure. Don Gaspar proved to be a much more conciliatory person at home than on the stagecoach and admitted that he had thought a good deal about their discussion and wanted the young man to understand that he had great respect for his point of view. Abraham was delighted to accept the friendship offered to him and during the next few months he visited the house frequently and was always well-received by the master and courteously welcomed by the servants. He came to understand and to admire the old man who in turn showed growing affection for Abraham and frequently introduced him to members of rich and influential local families.

One bleak day in the preceding January, Abraham had been urgently called to see Don Gaspar who had become suddenly very ill and was likely to die. He had gone at once, saddened at the situation of one whom he now considered as a great friend. At the bedside, Don Gaspar told him that he had no other relatives, that he had for a long time regarded Abraham as his own son and that he proposed to bequeath to him his whole estate. He told Abraham that he must prepare himself for the responsibilities and obligations required of one dealing with a vast fortune and extensive properties. It was only the extreme youth of his heir that worried the dying man and he had the boy's promise that he would immediately seek out the family solicitor and would abide by his advice in all matters.

This Abraham did, acquainting Mr. Stanistreet of a well-known Liverpool firm of solicitors of Don Gaspar's death and putting all the dead man's affairs into the lawyer's hands. It was six long months after the funeral when Mr. Stanistreet came to Shrewsbury to see Abraham, with all matters of probate settled and with the information that the inheritance was of a total of something like half a million pounds. There were also family estates abroad. He also gave Abraham a good deal of advice, including the need to keep everything as quiet as possible. He feard that, because of Abraham's youth, there would be rogues and predators of all kinds eager to lay hands on the inheritance by one means or another. At his suggestion they placed all the relevant documents in an iron chest and together buried it at an agreed spot on the estate. Only they knew where it was hidden. Abraham concluded his account by saying that he had tried to keep the whole affair secret since Don Gaspar had asked him to say nothing until the New Year.

John Cawston listened to his son's story lost in an amazement that robbed him of speech. To the simple farmer it was a tale as improbable as Aladdin and his lamp, yet there was a confidence in the boy and a certain logical consistency in all the details that somehow had the mark of truth. In a kind of daze, he found himself agreeing to keep the matter secret for the time being.

Such an extraordinary matter could not rest, however. John Cawston spent a number of long, sleepless nights weighing up all the strange aspects of the story, unwilling by nature to believe anything that savoured of nonsense but equally unwilling to think that Abraham could or would tell what was untrue. In the end he confessed to Abraham that the problem was so heavy in his mind that he felt he must ask the advice of his friend Mr. Weatherall, a prominent solicitor in Shrewsbury. Abraham agreed that he saw his father's difficulty and offered to accompany him to the interview. There, he begged Mr. Weatherall to make the most complete investigation that he felt was merited in order to ease his father's mind. The solicitor was impressed by the boy's good sense and concern for others and promised to look into the matter at once.

Some days later, John Cawston met the solicitor walking in the town and asked him if he had made any progress.

'Well,' answered Mr. Weatherall, 'I haven't had time to

go into it at all thoroughly but I must say that I think everything about your son's story rings true. I am sure you have nothing to feel doubtful about. He is a sensible boy anxious not to hurry his affairs too quickly but I have no doubt myself that he is sitting on a fortune.'

It was good enough for the farmer, who straight away apologised to his son for apparently doubting him. Seeing that he was convinced, Abraham then calmly gave him a list of the amounts and sources of the wealth which had accrued from Don Gaspar's dealings in diamonds. Many of his most valuable gems had gone to royal houses, some of which were deeply in his debt. Repayments of these debts and income from other sources were to be paid to Abraham at half yearly intervals, the first due on January 5th. On that day, but not before, Abraham would come into his own and prove with hard cash his exalted position.

During the autumn that preceded that notable day, a host of people became busy in involving themselves in a variety of ways with the wealthy-to-be Cawston family, now that the secret was out. Bankers and financiers with their attendant lawyers on one side, society people with invitations and county people with marriageable daughters on the other, threatened to engulf the routine of farming life. Nearly everyone had a proposition to make and as the rumours of Abraham's wealth expanded so each proposition seemed to be more grandiose than the one before. The boy must live in a style suited to his great fortune. He must have fine clothes, a carriage and horses, above all a country seat of impressive size. Lawyers would arrange for him to become a ward of Chancery and later he could enter politics by purchasing a number of parliamentary boroughs which would bring such power to his elbow as to lead him directly to a title. As a man of title it would be his privilege to assume a more commanding name. Devereux sounded very good. The College of Heralds would design the insignia for the name Devereux.

During all this feverish excitement Abraham remained calm and committed to his usual sober habits. When others

62

were inclined to celebrate he took little part but devoted more and more time to his papers and business matters. Occasionally, important looking documents were to be seen on his desk, some bearing the heading of the de Quintilla estate, some having the seal of some bank. It was a natural gesture of a fond uncle of Abraham's to press upon him a round sum of twelve hundred pounds to allow him elbow room until his January receipts arrived and Mr. Weatherall demonstrated his own faith in the young heir by bestowing a further sixteen hundred pounds. Abraham accepted the sums with reluctance but made it clear that he would not take advantage of any other of the many kind offers that were made to him. His needs, he pointed out, were really very few.

Nevertheless, the tide of aggrandizement began to sweep the boy forward. He agreed, under persuasion, that he should seek out a residence and estate appropriate to a person of great wealth. On October 24th, 1817, John Cawston caused an advertisement to appear in the Cambridge *Chronicle and Journal* requesting information about such a property.

'Any Gentleman wishing to dispose of an eligible Freehold Estate in the counties of Norfolk, Suffolk, Essex or Cambridgeshire, may hear of a purchaser, by applying to Mr. Cawston, Chippenham, Cambs. Value from 150 to 200,000 pounds. Principals only dealt with.'

The most eligible freehold estate that turned up was the grand residence of Houghton Hall in Norfolk that had been built for Robert Walpole. Without delay, John Cawston began to take the preliminary steps to negotiations for the purchase. It seemed right, at the same time to engage a retinue of servants including a valet and a secretary. Excitement mounted as December arrived and Abraham could not avoid a host of invitations and propositions from all sides. In return, he was sometimes host to a gathering of would-be friends or of neighbours at the farmhouse, when he would put aside all the plans and business matters for a time to take a leading if abstemious part in the celebrations.

One such jolly affair consisted of a number of local farmers and friends who were happy to join the select band within the aura of great wealth and were intrigued to know that they were to be asked their opinions on a Sicilian wine imported from Abraham's own vineyards on the slopes of Mount Etna. If suitable for English palates, Abraham planned to open a market here for the wine.

The treachery of those envious of another's wealth is well known. Among the guests that evening was one who, though well provided with his host's generous measures of wine, could not quite drown a rankling suspicion. There had been quite a performance of passing wine bottles among the company and this man spotted a single dis-carded cork that carried a printed name. He was curious enough, next day, to seek out the owner of the name, a prominent London vintner. Yes, the bottles of wine had been bought at that establishment.

Perhaps a man of more charitable disposition might have assumed that a simple mistake had been made or that Abraham had merely been guilty of a minor deception. Instead, the suspicious one dug more deeply into the matter. Through the vintner and from foreign sources he discovered that not only had the wine not come from the de Quintilla estates in Sicily, there were no de Quintilla estates in Sicily. Nor were there any de Quintilla estates in France or Germany or Spain as there were supposed to be.

Worse still, there was no such person as Gaspar de Quintilla nor a friendly solicitor nor buried documents nor any fortune. Before the bubble broke, which would have been bound to happen on January 5th anyway, Abraham found himself pressingly required to attend to business abroad, and with secretary and valet in attendance, dis-appeared from all knowledge.

In a way, it was the most extensive, inflated confidence trick ever conceived but there are features of the story that preclude such a banal conclusion. To be sure, Abraham's uncle and Mr. Weatherall were worse off to the total of about £2800 but no one else suffered unduly from the exercise. If it were only a scheme for profit, the sheer size and importance of the operation could have secured him a much greater return than these relatively unimportant sums. His reserved attitude and limited gains seem to speak of a runaway imagination rather than cupidity. Having started the hare of untold wealth he could scarcely withdraw from the hunt. The whole idea seems to have arisen from that original puzzle — the question of his excessive pocket money at Shrewsbury School. His agile imagination invented a cover-up that required a continued deception until the inevitable show-down. The nagging question remains . . . from where did the pocket money come?

James Murrell — Wizard

There should be some consolation to those of us who bemoan the imperfections of the modern world that at least we are removed by a century or so and a high degree of scepticism from the power of wizards and witches. We pretend now that such people never existed and we put them away very neatly with their conical tall hats and broomsticks into childish fairy tales and laugh at the very idea. Yet in the first half of the last century they still flourished in flesh-and-blood individuals, as influential among the simple people of the countryside as any priest or doctor. One such was James Murrell, now considered to be probably the last practising wizard in the country. Like many of his kind, he was generally referred to as a Cunning Man. Cunning he certainly was, that little man who wielded such power in quite a largish corner of Essex. He was no more than five feet tall, as quick as a fox and as sharp as a weasel. There was very little about the fallibility of man or of animals that he did not know.

James Murrell, the Cunning Man of Hadleigh in Essex, lived in an environment so apt to his profession that it must at least have contributed to his reputation, if it did not in the first place convert him to his life of mystery and supernatural power. Flat, low marshes and dykes, where once the famous painter Constable came to try to transfer the lonely magic of the place to canvas, where mists were a regular part of the landscape and sometimes enveloped everything in veils of mystery, sometimes created ghostly shapes that seemed to rise out of the ground. There he lived, in a small, isolated shack far away from the highway and it made a weird and gloomy journey for the many troubled mortals who came to seek his help. The hut was tarred black and the walls inside and out were hung with many kinds of herbs as well as less attractive examples of local wild life. Close by and the only sign that any other habitation had ever existed here, were the ruins of a Norman castle, long since occupied by nothing but murky shadows.

From these surroundings Murrell shaped and encouraged the flow of local superstition into eminently profitable channels and so successful was he in the weird and awe-inspiring machinations of wizardry that troubled people from far and near came to beat a path to his door. It was a perfect backcloth for his consummate use of superstition to aid his many devious and deep-rooted schemes. No wonder that, though brought up to be a shoemaker, he soon renounced that humble trade.

Perhaps the most regular of Murrell's daily chores was in divining the future for those who were love-lorn or merely curious, though this was a mere bread-and-butter business compared to the vast range of his activities. More important was his power to withstand the witches and many believed that he was the only person who could counteract their spells. Witches abounded in the area — there were said to be nine in the next village alone — and there was much admiration and inevitable profit for the Cunning Man in his power to release worried villagers from afflictions derived from an evil eye.

More spectacularly successful was Murrell's record in the matter of recovering lost or stolen property, particularly of farm animals. Losing the whereabouts of a horse or a cow in the open marshes could easily happen and farmers wasted no more time than necessary in searching the dykes and ditches but went hot-foot to the black-tarred hut for assistance. In his capacity as wizard, the Cunning Man would know everything that was happening in the area and was able to recover the animals with amazing ease. Grateful farmers would scarcely have had time to pay the required fee in advance before the horse or cow would turn up again in their own stockyard. If anyone ever had a glimmer of doubt about such incidents or about any other of Murrell's activities, they were reminded of the essential mystery of magic, of his constant battles with the witches and the difficulties of wresting stolen property away from them.

Less well known was Murrell's interest in events in the river estuary or even in the Thames on certain moonlit nights when a load of contraband was due to arrive. Moonlight, in fact, often kept him company out-of-doors while law-abiding folk lay abed, for if not engaged in nefarious business with the smugglers he would be dashing off on some other mysterious errand like a will-o'-the-wisp of the marshes. He could travel long distances at night so fast that wondering villagers would swear that he was sometimes in two places at once. Often he was simply engaged in the mundane collecting of herbs which he vowed only retained their essential virtue if picked by moonlight. It was a regular chore for Murrell, conscientiously undertaken, and it shows him to be not completely a mountebank. There were many who certainly benefited from his ministrations in the sphere of herbal medicine and were ready to say so. His renowned nostrums were made with a genuine knowledge of the properties of plants and his treatment of disorders, whether in humans or animals, was successful enough to bring him sufferers from far¨nd wide. He charged the common round sum of one penny for all his compounds and was known to sell as many as forty nostrums in one day.

Country folk who made the pilgrimage to Murrell's squat, black hut in the marshes to ask for a herbal mixture to cure some ailment that he would swear had been put upon them by the witches, or to seek a love-potion or some other of the diverse reasons for their visits, were fascinated and somewhat awe-struck on being invited to enter. For one thing, there was revealed in flesh and blood the daughter of the wizard, Alice Murrell, who was seen so rarely abroad that many people insisted that she did not exist at all. But here she would be, rather silent and forbidding-looking but busy and sensible enough in the role of housekeeper and support for her father. She was touching middle age and had never married, since no local man would be prepared to ally himself with that family of unknown power and mystery. Not that Alice had any pretensions to special knowledge beyond her domestic duties. She would take the visitors silently past the rows of objects and plants essential to wizardry and introduce them into a small, inner room, somehow rather close and awesome. There they would come face to face with the Cunning Man, all five feet nothing of him, but with some assumed height and importance from wearing a frock coat with gold buttons and a very tall hard hat.

Of all the objects in the room calculated to strike fear and respect in the heart of the visitor, the most important was a piece of apparatus which Murrell would assure anyone inquisitive enough to ask was a machine designed to see through brick walls or through any other kind of solid object. It was a clever disposition of two telescopes and a series of small mirrors. If someone looked into one of the telescopes and placed their hand or some other opaque object over the other end, they could apparently look right through the obstacle as if it were not there. The practical value of this equipment may have been very small but as an advertisement of mystic power it had an impact far beyond the neighbourhood of Hadleigh. The thought that the wizard could look into any cottage at will through his strange eye-pieces was a chilling thought for vilage adults and children alike.

Another object conspicuous in the hut was a metal container something like a bottle in shape with an open end which could be stopped with a cork. It played an important part in the ritual when someone came with a problem difficult to solve because it was under a particularly strong spell of the witches. The degree of solemnity with which the container was used no doubt accorded closely to the size of the fee which the client was prepared to pay. The bottle would be filled with a compound of materials suitable to the particular problem and might

69

include the parings of horses' hoofs, kindly supplied by the blacksmith, sundry small objects like pins or needles, some pinches of mysterious chemicals and appropriate herbs. Murrell would take the container along to the blacksmith who would close the end by welding the metal. It would then be put on the forge fire and no doubt all those interested would retreat for a few minutes since the bottle was likely to explode. If this did happen the wizard would claim a victory since it indicated that the power of the witches was broken. Sometimes it happened that the bottle did not explode but only fizzled and spluttered impotently in the embers. Then the wizard would shake his head and declare that he could not solve the problem.

How extensive was Murrell's exercise of a Cunning Man's powers was discovered when, at his death, a whole sack-full of letters was found in his lonely shack, sent by people all over East Anglia and some even from London. Some of the contents of the letters were of bizarre matters as seen by modern eyes, telling of such things as evil spirits and ghostly persecution and of the devilry of witches. Others were from young women in similar pre-dicaments to those that seem to be perennial — of vanished sweethearts and unhappy homes and unwanted babies — an amalgam of misfortunes. Yet in the tone of the letters there was always a confidence that, even though all else may have failed, the Cunning Man would find a solution. No doubt that he sometimes did succeed where others had failed for he was certainly a most dedicated wizard. In those particular circumstances and at that particular time he filled a place that was important in the community.

When Murrell was finally forced to take to his bed after a long spell of activity he spoke to Alice of his fatigue and his wish that he should not be bothered again by anyone. In the stuffy keeping-room of the hut, Alice tended her father and kept importunate clients away for the few days of his illness. By her own account there was a remnant of magic in the manner of his death, for having set his affairs in order as well as he might, he declared that he was ready to die and would do so at one o'clock the following day. Next morning Alice counted the chimes of Hadleigh church clock as the time mounted to mid-day and exactly as it broke the silence again with the single bell of one o'clock, the last of the wizards died.

Margaret Catchpole — Heroine

If Richard Cobbold's book on the adventures of Margaret Catchpole were only romantic fiction it would still stir the emotions and hold the reader in thrall. To know that the story is largely true gives it an even greater fascination and for those of us who live in East Anglia there is the bonus of being able to identify local places as they were seen in the latter years of the eighteenth century. It is a book widely known and its heroine's name is as famous — perhaps for the wrong reasons — as any other who has seen the shadow of the hangman's rope. Cobbold's account of this extraordinary life is embellished to some degree from his own vivid imagination and there is no doubt that he had a strong sense of the visually dramatic. Since he is really the only authority on this Suffolk maid, one has to guess where fact begins to knit so charmingly with fancy. He does not hesitate, for example, to give complete word-by-word accounts of the lovers' conversations though no one on earth could possibly have overheard. His dialogue is shrewdly based on the character he knew well, since Margaret was a trusted servant in his mother's house and often confessed her troubles to the Cobbold family.

Upon her character all the strange events devolved — a character at the same time complex and yet simple, modest and yet ardent. Many of those who accused her in her darkest hour stayed to wonder at her straightforward honesty. Others spoke of her sensitivity and percipience far beyond the consciousness of ordinary folk and others, too, of her bravery and resolution. Certainly there was an emotional energy in her that could not be bound to the limited circumstances of her peasant life and would have been expressed in some form or other. But that it was directed for so long in a tragic loyalty to one who had no virtues of his own with which to respond, was an unhappy chance for which she had to pay dearly.

Margaret was the youngest child but one of a farm worker's family of six. He was the head horseman on a farm beside the river Orwell at Nacton, between Ipswich and Felixstowe. Horses were bred on the farm and Margaret shared her father's love for the majestic Suffolk Punch horses that she rode with great ease and enjoyment from her earliest days. In common with all her family she had no learning and could not read or write until she set herself to the task of self-education as a young woman.

An example of Margaret's quick wit and resolution occurred when she was just thirteen. She had gone to a neighbouring farmhouse with a message to deliver, in time to see the mistress fall in a fit and the servant girls squealing helplessly beside her. She settled the woman as comfortably as possible, gave instructions to the servants and told them that she must go to fetch a doctor. Running to the stable, she found only one horse available, a young and lively Punch with no harness but a halter around its neck. In an instant she was on its back and it was in this style, without saddle or bridle, her skirts and her hair flying in the wind, that she galloped the six miles or so into the town, much to the astonishment of the lookers-on.

The doctor drove out at once with Margaret beside him in the buggy and her horse following behind. Soon he had treated the woman, who quickly recovered and both she and the doctor were much taken with this young lass who had shown such initiative. The doctor, indeed, became Margaret's revered and trusted friend and many a time came to her aid when troubles were thick about her. As for Margaret, it was one of the most exciting rides of her life and she often looked back on that day with pleasure.

She was only about fourteen when she first met Will Laud and for the next fifteen years of Margaret's life the dominating theme was her strong and constant attachment to the headstrong young smuggler. One might well think that it was a very unrewarding devotion for they seldom met; Laud was often at sea or away on some illicit adventure and when he did appear it was to bring guilt and trouble and very little unalloyed joy. To be sure he sent her gifts but these were smuggled goods that only brought pain and disrepute to the family and Margaret would keep none of them. Yet her loyalty to him was such that in most matters she followed whatever dangerous trails he laid down for her. Thoughts of wrong-doing or of punishment did not matter. Nothing, until he was shot dead by her side after her escape from prison, could deter her for a moment from her single-minded devotion. By that time she had seen her whole family destroyed through the influence of the smuggler, through grief and drink and dishonour, their former simple lives tainted by Laud's reputation.

Of all the features of this unhappy and one-sided love affair the most notorious was Margaret's epic ride to London on a stolen horse. Tricked into believing that Laud was waiting for her there and that they were to be married, Margaret took the horse from the stables of her employer at Ipswich and accomplished the journey at a breakneck speed. When she reached London, there was only bitter disappointment. Laud was not there, she realised that she had been deceived and, since she was penniless, she offered the horse for sale. Almost at once she was arrested, taken initially to Newgate but then brought back to Suffolk to be tried for the heinous crime of horse stealing. For all the efforts of the Cobbolds, the doctor and other friends she was sentenced to death. Had she divulged the reason for that dramatic ride the court may well have been more lenient but she kept secret the facts that might have implicated Laud and was treated as a common horse thief. In the last hours the sentence was commuted to seven years imprisonment.

Sympathy for Margaret was widespread and it was likely that she would have gained an early release from prison but that her infatuation for the smuggler led her into another bizarre adventure. A suggestion from him that he would give up smuggling if she would join him in escaping to some foreign land caused her to compound her wrong-doing with a feat still to be marvelled at. With an extraordinary agility and strength as well as some cunning, she achieved an unaided break-out from the prison, among other obstacles having to scale a 22 feet high wall surmounted by an array of iron spikes.

Perhaps this time Laud really meant what he promised, for he soon caught up with her and the couple fled together. It was a desperate ill-planned flight and doomed to failure from the start. Soon after they had crossed the Deben by the Woodbridge ferry to the northern side, the police caught up with them. Laud resisted when called upon to surrender and was shot and killed beside the heart-broken girl. Margaret was tried again and sentenced to death for the second time. After consideration, the sentence was reduced to transportation for life.

But these are the wild and drastic episodes of Margaret's life and they reveal but a part of that young woman's complex disposition. Look, for instance, at the portrait that Richard Cobbold painted of her when she was in his employ and which now hangs in the Christchurch Museum in Ipswich. This is the picture of a demure and proper young woman who has applied care and strong principle to the bringing up of her mistress's children. It is the true likeness of a servant girl whose work has always been thorough to a degree and whose solicitude for her employer's family was never failing. On three occasions her prescience of danger and carelessness of her own safety allowed her to save a child from almost certain death. She became a treasured servant and in return for her loyalty gained the respect and affection of the Cobbold household.

It was this self-effacing demeanour and her ingenuous replies that silenced the witnesses at her trial. There was a kind of impregnable innocence in her attitude that was compared to that of the Maid of Orleans at her trial. The court was entranced at this confrontation with complete honesty. Given the invitation of a sympathetic judge to plead 'Not Guilty', she replied:

75

'I am not able, my lord, to plead "Not Guilty".'

'Why not?'

'Because I know that I am guilty.'

The judge was deeply troubled after sentencing her to death, spoke of her often and visited the prison from which she escaped. 'I wish I knew more of this woman,' he said. 'I could then judge things which appear inexplicable in such a person. Whence does she gain such power of speech, such simplicity of manners?'

Margaret's feelings at the trial seemed to be those of distress but rather because of the judge's harsh opinions than because of the sentence, to which she was quite resigned. Indeed, when the punishment was reduced to transportation for life, she begged for the original sentence to be upheld.

Margaret arrived at Sydney in the prison ship, the *Nile*, in December 1801, having been six months on the voyage. She had set out from England in deepest pessimism but during the voyage her usual readiness to respond to the needs of others kept her busy caring for the sick and dealing with the crises of close confinement. When the Governor came aboard at Sydney her reputation as a capable and sympathetic woman was already known and she was immediately taken into the domestic service of Mrs. Palmer, wife of the Commissary-General in New South Wales.

The notorious young horse-thief and felon, as a hand-bill had once referred to her, was now 28 years old and had another 40 years of life ahead of her. Gradually she took to the forthright Australian people who asked no questions of her past and was surprised at the agreeable climate. In time her yearning for her home and friends beside the Orwell diminished, though not her affection for her former mistress, Mrs. Cobbold. In those early years on the other side of the world it was Margaret's greatest interest to collect what she could of the skins or feathers of the exotic wild creatures of the colony and pack them up to send back to England. It seemed to give her an almost childish delight in being able to show her gratitude to the Cobbolds in this way and she was very cast down when one of the packages was lost. In return, Mrs. Cobbold sent regular parcels of small articles of domestic use which she shrewdly guessed would be very welcome in that wild, new country. To collect one of these parcels Margaret once walked the 50 miles to Sydney in two days, fortunately getting a lift back, since the terrain was almost entirely rough bush country. It was with the articles from some of the parcels, mainly of haberdashery that, years later, she opened a small shop for the settlers.

Her new mistress, Mrs. Palmer, was a friendly woman who did much to make Margaret's position more tolerable. For her part, Margaret was steadily gaining a reputation as one to whom the settlers and serving convicts alike could turn to in times of domestic emergency. The calm resolution and common sense that she had shown at Nacton when she was a young girl served her in good stead now when expert help could be a hundred miles or more away. After leaving Mrs. Palmer, who reluctantly allowed her to go, Margaret moved for some years among the scattered homes of settlers where their gratitude and her keep was payment enough for her services. Many called her the Nurse and declared that she was just as good as a doctor. When she was able to have a small home of her own, Margaret grew herbs and studied their uses and with her little bag of home-made cures became a figure as well-known as any in the province. In an emergency she would even perform minor surgery, by no means unthinkable in those early days of the wild new country where violence and hardship were a part of life. In the bad years when floods followed months of drought, Margaret exhausted herself in rescuing neighbours and friends in danger of losing not only their homes but their lives. There is a report of a specific incident when she dived into rushing flood waters to rescue a young boy whose make-shift raft had caught in a fallen tree.

At last the long-awaited full pardon arrived and Margaret had no longer to fret over the stigma of her conviction. She was nearly forty when she married a respectable settler and gained a family of three children. These were quieter, happier years in which she showed deep affection for her husband and was heart-broken when he died.

In her later years, she used to sit on the porch of her comfortable small house and look out towards the open bush country that had become so familiar to her. In her musings she must often have returned again to the days of her girlhood at Nacton, so far away and long ago. She must have remembered sometimes the excitement of the running of smuggled goods and the fights and the sound of guns and the thrill of hearing Will Laud's voice. She would remember, too, the pain and the ecstasy of that love affair that had cost her so dear and she would know that in the end she had been right because she had been true.

Marsham — The Tree Man

In a part of the country that has produced many distinguished naturalists and in a century noted for the laying
out of great estates by wealthy landowners it would be
difficult to show Robert Marsham as being any more
prominent than the rest, save in one particular — his
inordinate love for and affinity with his trees. No Johnny
Appleseed ever planted them so assiduously or watched
their growth with so much concern and pride. Trees were his
'mad-string' he confessed to his friend Gilbert White of
Selborne.

No doubt that trees occupy a varying degree of importance in everyone's life since they are not only the most
generous and beautiful expression of vegetative nature but
also extremely useful in their support of human life — too
amenable, in fact, for their own good. It only needs an axe
to bring two hundred years' of growth to a sudden end and
an adze to shape and carve the workable material into a
hundred uses from mere chairs to magnificent ships, from
barrel hoops to houses. As a bonus, the wooden article
carries with it the strong and handsome qualities that arise
from its origins in living power. The temptations of such
useful and easily available wealth to generations of exploi-
ters could well have made the whole earth a desert but for
the obstinacy of nature. Against the axe and the fire the tree
persists in surviving. How many may be left to enjoy their
full maturity is another matter.

I wonder if trees really fare much better in this age of
conservationists than they did in the centuries of exploitive
timber merchants. Conservationists are largely drawn from
those ranks of people who have migrated from the towns to
the countryside since the war. They demonstrate a vocal
interest in trees and hedges but the concern they show is
superficial, a kind of cause without much real knowledge or

dedication. Many of these people who come into the countryside to live find it initially charming and then rather untidy so they set about showing the natives how to tidy it up, often by cutting down the trees near to their houses because the leaves are such a nuisance in the autumn. The thought that the leaf may be the basis of their existence does not stir their conscience in the matter.

Compare this rather abstract interest in trees with the respect shown by the simple natives of East Anglia of only a hundred years ago. Then there were individual trees as famous as human notables, their names known far and wide. Homage was paid to them by visits paid on long Sunday walks, with a picnic, perhaps, in the shade of the spreading branches. At Bury St. Edmunds, for example, there was the Abbot's Willow, reputed to be 700 years old and the even more admirable Black Poplar that stood by the river Lark. It was 90 feet high and for half that height the circumference of the trunk did not vary an inch — a perfect column of immense proportions. Among others, there was the famous Kirby Oak at Shrubland Park near Ipswich and the Monk Soham Oak said to be planted by monks in the Middle Ages. At Bungay there was the wonder of the H trees, two elms linked by a horizontal branch just a yard from the ground. But who would walk to see them now?

In the eighteenth century, trees occupied an important place in the laying out of great estates and Robert Marsham was among the favoured landowners rich enough to plan a modest estate for himself. His tree-planting, however, went far beyond the usual pictorial requirement of statuesque specimens. His interest was detailed and personal and unremitting. He was hungry for trees and for land that would accommodate more trees and to the end of his life the hunger was not satisfied. Marsham saw a tree as a day-to-day miracle, a continuing revelation that never waned. The conception of a tree as a semi-permanent thing since it spans longer than a human life and shows little spectacular change was heresy to him. He believed that a tree profited by constant attention and always rewarded the owner for the extra care. It was an attitude that needed a great deal of patience, an absorbing interest in nature and a long life. Robert Marsham was fortunate enough to be given all three of these attributes.

Robert was born in 1708, the eldest son of a prominent family long established at Stanton Strawless in Norfolk. His interest in natural history began with his earliest years and at ten years old he was not only beginning to keep his life-long records of spring changes but was also planting acorns and conkers and beech-nuts, an occupation that he came to be grateful for in the latter years of his life. Above all others of his trees he cherished a particular oak that he had planted as an acorn and a Spanish chestnut also grown from seed, which had grown along with Robert and accompanied him through the years to their common maturity.

He was twenty years old when he became a scholar of Cambridge University and it was about this time that he formed a lasting friendship with William Wyndham and his tutor Benjamin Stillingfleet, each to become well-known in other aspects of Norfolk life but at that time intensely interested in botanical studies. After Cambridge and some travelling with his friends, Robert settled down on his father's estate as a young squire and forthwith began his exhaustive observations that he called Indications of Spring. Each year he made detailed notes on the first appearences of wild flowers, bird's nests, butterflies and bud-break in all the varied species of trees, together with all the other minute signs that presage the yearly awakening. Thanks to his consistent interest, the project was followed without a break for sixty years and formed the basis of the valuable records which he — and later, Stillingfleet — presented to the Royal Society.

The Marsham estate was not large by some eighteenth century standards but it followed the general intentions of richer landowners in extending the landscape vistas by the planting of trees. It was never enough for young Marsham, more acres had to be planted, new groves added, neighbouring fields acquired so that his ruling passion could be indulged. Much of the soil of the original estate was light and poor and here he planted pine and spruce but his favourites were oak and beech and Spanish chestnut and he used these to mask the soft woods. On the better soils he planted ten varieties for the purpose of his detailed records — oak, beech, chestnut, elm, Scots pine, pinaster, larch, spruce and willow — and in the persuance of all the practical and experimental work associated with these, his life was fully absorbed. The rate of growth of different trees in different situations was a matter of endless concern and he would make frequent measurements, in some cases at least once a month during the growing season.

Robert's feeling of close affinity with his trees only increased as he became older and they became ever more demanding of his attention. He was diverted for no more than a moment by his marriage to Mary Browne of Yaxham and no more than a trifle again when his father died two years later. He was now in complete charge of the estate and he filled his days with planting, and pollarding, coppicing and thinning, according to the season. In the grove of trees he loved best he built himself a small hut that was thatched with reeds and very soon covered with ivy and in this shelter he would sit for hours on end, always absorbed by the wonders of growth and development. Here, when about thirty years old, he planted tiny cedars round about and was able to see over fifty years' growth on them before he died.

When not occupied with observing and Note-taking in his quiet arbour, he busied himself with the more practical tasks required for the proper care of woodland and soon became known as an expert in methods of pollarding and thinning. Any new ideas from other arborists, especially on the subject of increasing the rate of growth, he seized on avidly for this was his interest above all others. For many years he cleared and strenuously dug all around the bases of some of the trees to ascertain if this had a beneficial effect. When a fellow naturalist, Dr. Stephen Hales, propounded the theory that the washing of the trunks of trees would surely have a marked effect on growth, Robert Marsham eagerly began a series of controlled experiments whose results were noted in detail and sent to the Royal Society.

Following Dr. Hales' recommendations, he would choose single specimens that were typical of a group and set to with the simple equipment of a stiff shoe brush and pails of clean, cold water. The tree trunk would be thoroughly washed and brushed to clean the crevices of moss and other fungus as far up as the lowest branches. There would be several washes a week all through the summer and always accompanied by the inevitable measuring and recording. The results achieved were so good that Robert extended his ministrations from his favourite beeches to oaks and other species.

Such close care of his charges and the need to note the progress of all his experiments kept him engrossed throughout the day and often into the night as well. Ladders were an inevitable part of his activities and it was William Wyndham, who, having watched the arborist clambering up and down trees at all hours and in all kinds of weather, expressed the belief that 'Marsham will dye off of a ladder.' Even on a dark night without moon or stars, Wyndham complained to his friend Stillingfleet, the man would be lost in a tree somewhere, perched sixteen or twenty feet above the ground and completely unaware of his obligations elsewhere. While such peculiar habits could be indulgently accepted by his naturalist friends, by the prosaic farmers and cottagers of the neighbourhood the matter was inevitably seen with considerable amusement. Washing a tree was the funniest thing that they had heard of in all their experience on the land and each new snippet of news relayed from workers on the estate produced many a guffaw when there was little else to laugh about.

As time went on, the study of his trees took all Robert's time and attention, exceeding even his regular observations of Spring harbingers, which Stillingfleet took over with great success in the year 1755. Most pampered and treasured of all were the two old friends — the oak and the Spanish chestnut — that were shown without fail to every visitor. Marsham's long-suffering wife was driven almost to distraction by the situation. Conversations with someone in a tree, particularly if that someone was completely absorbed in arboreal matters were not very productive, she found and she was particularly anxious to discuss other and what seemed to her more important subjects. There was the promised new house, for example. Surely it should not be beyond her husband's recollection that in the euphoric early days of their marriage he had promised to engage in the building of a new and more commodious house on the estate. After all, the plans had been made, everyone had been enthusiastic about the idea, especially William Wyndham and Benjamin Stillingfleet, who were themselves architects.

It had soon become clear, however, that Robert's real interest in the project extended no further than considering the kinds of trees that would embellish the site. To be sure, he agreed to the plans and the situation and even went so far as to make a quantity of bricks for the structure but his enthusiasm was only for the avenues of oak, beech and lime that he would plant at the approaches to the Hall. As the years passed the trees flourished but the avenues pointed to nowhere but a good intention . . . Each year his wife would endeavour to persuade him of the advantages to be secured from a superior dwelling and from time to time he would earnestly resolve to get something done. Yet whenever there was money to spare there was sure to be another stretch of land that he needed to buy to accommodate ever more trees. For the next forty years of his life the trees grew and the site languished. It was not until after his death that his son, a baby when the idea had first been proposed, had the house built at last.

During the latter part of that forty years, Marsham had happily engaged himself in a constant exchange of letters with the distinguished naturalist, Gilbert White of Selborne. He must have regretted often that he had not come across White's *History of Selbourne* earlier for they were both old men when Robert wrote his initial letter in praise of the book. At once a shared and almost brotherly concern for a common cause sprang up between the two and from the

84

regular correspondence that followed it is difficult to tell which of them was more delighted. Comparisons of their records of observations and the fascination of natural life in general actually inspired Robert to recall his earlier and wider interests and though there was no doubt an emphasis on trees in his letters, the experience was a happy one for both. Though Gilbert White had only three more years to live and the two men never had the opportunity to meet, Robert Marsham regarded the association as being one of the most important things in his life.

In his old age, with a second wife to endure his strange love of trees, he continued in remarkably good health and with no abatement of enthusiasm. If he climbed ladders less frequently than before and reduced his scope of observations and experiments, he still followed the chosen pattern of his life right up to his ninetieth year, a dispensation for which he was duly grateful. In 1780 his work on the recording of growth in trees earned him a Fellowship of the Royal Society, a fact which by no means persuaded him that his practical work was over for at the age of eighty five he was setting out once more on the planting of a new wood. He must have been sadly conscious that he would never accompany these new plantings beyond the stripling stage and that someone else must soon take over their care. After a long winter that drained his strength but not his resolution, he wrote to a relative — 'My Physicians tell me that my symptoms are not mortal and I think forward with pleasure that before May I may hobble with my crutches and admire some of my favourite trees.'

Most admired of all, to the very end, was his favourite oak, his stalwort contemporary that had grown from the acorn of childhood and was now of a majestic size with a trunk twelve and a half feet in circumference. This friend, and all the others he had cared for during his whole life, he had at last to leave behind.

John Elwes — Miser

The day that the new squire arrived in the village of Stoke-by-Clare was one of widespread rejoicing. At last the old squire was dead. May God rest his soul, the villagers prayed, but let us also smile a little at his going, for we have not smiled much during his lifetime. There are not many, even among the most saintly, who can find the charity to forgive a miser or to mourn a dedicated misanthrope. Old Sir Hervey could be numbered among the basest of these.

Now that he was dead, the long years of calculated skimping and penny-pinching would surely come to an end. Accordingly, faces put on a new and unaccustomed cheeriness to greet the newcomer. From cottage door and hay field, from mill yard and smithy, the welcome was genuine and heart-felt. There was a confident whisper abroad that the new John Elwes was a man with an open hand and a ready understanding of estate problems, someone who, at this moment and under these circumstances, came as much as a saviour for the village as a squire at the Hall. The knowledge that he was not a direct descendent of the Elwes family but had only taken the name for convenience sake, endeared him the more.

Times would change, neighbours told each other, adding the observation that they could only change for the better, for no one else could ever be so oppressively mean as the old man. When they gathered for a gossip and a stoup of ale at the inn they could even afford to laugh and recall how each of them had suffered from the dead squire's idiosyncrasies, jubilant that they were now beyond his reach.

After all, he had been at the Hall so long that the oldest man in the village could not remember the time when, child or man, Hervey Elwes had not been there. He would have been over eighty when he died, they reckoned and most of that long life spent in miserable seclusion. Everyone had a story to tell of devious means he had used to with-hold the payment of money to workers, tradesmen and shopkeepers and how, by dire economies he had managed to reduce his total expenditure to just one hundred and ten pounds a year, which sum included the meagre wages of a manservant and two maids. For all that, it had been his prevailing obsession that he must cut that amount still further and he had been known to go to extraordinary lengths to avoid the loss of a single penny from his vast fortune.

With such a stingy outlook on the estate's affairs, it was no wonder that the idea of capital expenditure had long been discounted as improbable by the tenants. Promises of renovations were subject to such indefinite delays that farmer and cottager alike learned to repair as best they could from their own resources. The Hall itself was a prime example of what such economy could do, since it declined to something like a ruin within the old man's lifetime. Rain entered freely from a dozen leaks in the roof and mould grew on damp walls while dust accumulated in the attics. Windows that became broken were patched with odd pieces of glass or stuffed with paper. Yet Sir Hervey would have no fire save in the bitterest weather and grudged a candle to light his miserable existence. Miserliness rules his life.

Perhaps it was his strange horror of spending or giving in any degree that made him view those dependent on him with distrust and displeasure. Since the manorial influence was still strong in rural East Anglia, the chill wind was felt by all within the Elwes demesne. Without encouragement of any kind, they worked without any great interest. Knowing the great wealth which the Elwes family undoubtedly possessed, they accepted the cheese-paring measures with varied degrees of resignation and rancour. There was little cheer for anybody while the old man lived.

Small wonder that smiles greeted the newcomer. Such was the feeling, that church bells and joyous festivities might have been appropriate had such things not been lost long ago in the general melancholy. As it was, the welcome was quietly hopeful when John Meggott, Sir Hervey's nephew, came at last to take up his inheritance of the broken-down Hall and the run-down estate. And, true to all expectations, changes were put in hand immediately. Fresh air and new ideas blew away the cobwebs in the corridors of the old house and in the empty barns. Farmers who had been used to buttressing their collapsing buildings with branches from trees were almost startled at the prospect of getting proper repairs at the squire's expense. Tradesmen, workers and tenants alike looked towards the Hall with new interest and sure enough it was not long before there were the cheerful sounds of industry about.

It was a heartening sign for the village and its future prosperity when the big house was renovated and the stables opened up again. Soon there were some fine horses for hunting, with grooms and stablemen to look after them. A magnificent carriage next made an appeerence, together with all the other appurtenances of a well-to-do gentleman. Indeed, at this time John was entertaining ambitions to shine in public service and stood for Parliament, eventually becoming an M.P. for a constituency in Berkshire. Obviously, too, a man of such public achievements and personal virtues was able to occupy an eminent place in the social circles of the county.

All seemed to be going well. The estate began to flourish again, the servants dared to sing in the kitchen and the peasant populace were ready enough to touch their forelocks when the squire's carriage went by.

Then, no sooner had this new order of confidence and trust been built up than it began to crumble. The attitude of the central figure on whom so many people's lives and prospects depended, slipped gradually from one of open generosity to one of introspection and suspicion. Old men shook their heads when they first noticed the change, thinking that there must be some ineradicable trait in the family to make this last member of the dynasty take what

88

seemed to be the same sad, stony road that others had taken. They remembered particularly the story of old Sir Hervey's mother, of long ago. That perfect model for all future Elwes misers had inherited a fortune of a hundred thousand pounds while still a young woman. During her lifetime the disease had taken such a hold on her that she seemed to endure an agony at the very thought of parting with money and in the end she starved herself to death rather than buy food.

Now they were to see the same sickness in the new squire. No one could say what caused the change or exactly when it came about but it was soon widely remarked that the generosity of the early years was in dwindling evidence. Increasingly, he showed concern at items of expenditure, then there were some accounts which received downright refusals. He was spending too much, he protested. He was 'too profuse'.

Very soon he was cutting expenditure in all departments and those familiar with the bad old days of his uncle's penny-pinching measures saw history repeating itself. There would be no turning back, they knew, once that family obsession had taken hold.

So, in fact, it turned out to be. Economies became more and more radical until every form of expense was cut to the bone. The sound of workmen around the house was no longer heard and in the barns only mice and the occasional owl stirred among the old beams. Parsimony ruled over all.

As time went by, John Elwes' tight-fisted ways earned the anger and opprobrium of all who had once praised him. He was, it was generally agreed, a skinflint ten times worse than his uncle had been. Once more the Hall deteriorated, became bare and gloomy, showed the rags of paper over broken windows and gaps in the roof where tiles were never replaced. All around were the signs of a dismal philosophy in which it was a sin to be 'too profuse'. Now, in the stable stood one visibly decrepit old mare in place of the four hunters once kept with pride. The squire rode her infrequently into the village and always kept to the soft turf at the side of the road in order to reduce the wear on the horse's shoes. Occasionally one or two of the erstwhile friends from John's more sociable days would drop in to try and jolly him out of his seclusion and their horses would wait for their owners in the stable. Useless it would be and risky of dire punishment for a stable boy of generous disposition to bestow a handful of hay upon the animals. If he suspected the boy of doing something so rash, the squire would be likely to excuse himself to his visitors and creep into the stable to take the fodder back.

Inside the Hall, John Elwes lived in the severe conditions that his niggardliness made inevitable. A fire was a rare luxury, to be grudged rather than enjoyed and if there was a fire in the kitchen made necessary for cooking he would go and sit with the servants there. When there was a hint of sun in the dark days of winter or early spring he would remove himself to the greenhouse to take advantage of the sun's warmth.

Even the spending of money on food was a constant regret. To avoid a bill from a butcher he would have a sheep killed and thenceforward eat nothing but mutton until the last morsel was done. By that time the carcase was usually showing signs of putrefaction but whatever qualms he felt about the condition of the meat were stilled by the strictest priority of his way of life that nothing must be wasted. In fact, to the end of his days he retained a good appetite and boasted a stomach that was completely accommodating as to the means of satisfying it. Among the more bizarre tales of his eating habits is that of his making a meal of part of a moorhen dragged from the river by a rat. Another repast that seemed to give him much satisfaction consisted of the undigested part of a pike that had been swallowed by another pike. 'Killing two birds with one stone,' he commented.

Perhaps it is only fair to remember that nothing excites exaggeration more than miserliness and it it possible that some of the tales of John Elwes' eccentricities could prove to be only excesses of their own kind. However, much of the evidence for such reports was unmistakeable and visible to all. His manner of dress, for example, was of such a kind that only a miser could contemplate with satisfaction. Each year as the house disintergrated about him, his clothes became similarly threadbare and piecemeal as he patched and strung together old garments. Boots and shoes had to last a long time and were never cleaned as he held that this helped to wear them out.

Out of doors, where dour farm workers rather than prattling servants looked on, he displayed the same horror of waste of all kinds, apparently without shame or embarrassment. As soon as the harvest was over he would go into the fields and glean for the remnants of fallen grain, alone and as tattered as a tramp in his ancient clothes. Among the tenant farmers it was an accepted ritual to humour his whims by throwing down a handful of corn here and there. When the winter came, he would walk the fields again to search along the hedgerows for broken boughs and sticks and even bones to carry back as fuel for the Hall.

For all that, John Elwes was a more complex character than many believe who simply seek to portray the arch-miser. Horses he loved and understood, perhaps better than he understood people, and when a young man had earned a reputation for being one of the most accomplished and daring riders in Europe. He was also for many years a member of the London club 'Arthur's' where he was frequently at the card tables and once completed a single unbroken session of gambling of two days and a night. Apparently he had no qualms about losing money in this way and it was once calculated that he must have lost something like £150,000 over a period of years, not so much from gambling as from speculations of many dubious sorts. Compared to the value of his many properties in central London, the losses were of no great importance. He also lost sums of money from frequent burglaries because of the general knowledge that he kept considerable amounts of cash in the house. One break-in alone cost him 2750 guineas.

John Meggott, or Elwes, never married but had two sons born of the housekeeper at his house at Marcham. Though apparently very fond of his sons, he resisted any ideas about educating them. 'Putting things into peoples' heads is the sure way to take money out of their pockets,' he used to quote. He himself had had a classical education but it was part of his odd life-style at Stoke-by-Clare that he never opened a book there, so far as anybody could tell.

He died in November 1789, leaving half a million pounds but to the end of his life he worried that he was 'too profuse.'

Ted Kittles — Vagrant

Perhaps the most surprising thing about Ted Kittles is that he survives at all in the saga of East Anglian notables. His contribution to contemporary life generally was minimal, his attitude and manners wayward to say the least and his hold on other peoples' patience and affections very tenuous. The best that can be said of him, perhaps, is that he was a child of circumstances, a victim of a prejudiced social order which kept him firmly under its thumb. Not that he was alone in such a situation by any means. The only thing that separates Ted from the army of paupers and beggars of his day is that he fought as hard for indolence and personal freedom as others did for virtuous conformity and that he defended his actions at every opportunity with a pertinent repartee which frequently silenced the authorities but earned himself widespread official disapprobation. For most of his lifetime he proved to be a thorn in the flesh of local big-wigs and among the under-dogs of the region his reputation flourished. In fact, the name of Kittles was already one for villagers to gawp and gossip over for his father had livened the environs of Cretingham to such an extent that the Crossways where he lived came to be known as Kittle's Corner.

Ted was born in Cretingham and brought up there but by the time of reaching manhood he was under the authority of Earl Soham parish as a pauper. The Poor Laws of the day were sadly lacking in the benevolence of later times. Pauperism was seen as a disreputable and expensive wart on the fair face of society. Awkward and recalcitrant paupers like Ted Kittles received the utmost opprobrium for their lack of gratitude and received very little sympathy when hauled before a magistrate or workhouse overseer.

At that time, the basis of provision for the poor lay in the responsibility of each parish for its own. Since parish purses were light, the local dispensers of aid were assiduous in counting the heads of those in need and if possible reducing the number. Simply persuading a local beggar to move on to another area would not work as he would be whipped and sent back to his proper parish. However, devious ideas were used by officials to reduce their payments to paupers.

One incident, associated with the same village of Earl Soham that Ted Kittles was later to illumine in his own manner, occurred one bright August morning when all, except paupers and vagrants, looked splendid in the rural scene. A local girl, who was in the legal care of the workhouse at Iken, walked along the road there and by chance met a young man trudging in the opposite direction. To Martha Stanton it was a heaven-sent opportunity. Only a few days before, the overseer had praised her good looks and told her that if she should get herself shortly married to someone outside he village and get taken off the rates it would be worth her while to the tune of five pounds to be paid over on her wedding day. Martha duly put the proposition to the stranger, Tom Collins, who as promptly accepted. On their wedding day, the overseer of the workhouse handed over the money and doubtless congratulated himself upon a fine bargain.

However, such methods were not likely to get rid of Ted Kittles. Projects to deal with him were frequently devised but never succeeded. He was hide-bound in a kind of innocence which people could never decide was real or posed. Cleverness on the part of authority was lost in his very stupidity. But surely, the overseer argued, with more hope than conviction, if they could not get rid of the man they could at least find him work so that he could earn his keep. No matter how simple he was, there were plenty of simple jobs to be done.

Stone-picking seemed to be the answer. Even such a fool as Ted Kittles could pick up stones — he couldn't do worse than a six-year-old, could he? The master from the Union set him to work one fine morning all on his own in the largest field in the village. When he returned later in the day to see

94

how the job was progressing, he found that Ted had picked up only the smooth stones, leaving the rough and jagged ones lying in the field.

'That won't do at all,' the master told him. 'All the stones have to be picked. Just take them as they come.'

Ted watched him go away, kept his eye on the stones for a time, then stretched out and went to sleep. When the master reappeared, he found that Ted had picked no more stones. Beyond patience, the master railed angrily. What was the use of a man sitting in the middle of a field doing nothing? Why hadn't he picked any stones? How could he expect other people to keep him if he did nothing in return?

'Well, master,' Ted is reported to have replied: 'you did say I was to take 'em as they come. So far there ain't none of 'em come.'

Taking Ted away from the stone-picking was only to invite other kinds of ineptitude, how much of it real and how much just craftily adopted can only be guessed. At first, turnip pulling seemed to be the sort of occupation about which mistakes could not possibly be made. You simply bent down, pulled the turnips out of the ground one after another and threw them down in a tidy row for others to collect up. The master explained it all very carefully and saw as a kind of triumph that Ted was actually pulling up turnips the way he was told.

After the master had gone, the routine continued for a few minutes, until a turnip with deeper roots momentarily resisted. After a good deal of contemplation though not much effort Ted decided that he could not proceed with the job until this obstacle was overcome. He therefore made himself comfortable until the master's return, having thoughtfully put a noose of cord over the offending turnip top with which he hoped the master would help to pull it free.

The irate master took him away from the problems of turnips and stones and tried to think of an even simpler task that Ted could be expected to do. Surely he could do no harm in digging a ditch? What could go wrong with such a simple operation as moving soil? In due course the master set him to work and had the satisfaction of seeing Ted apparently enjoying the exercise and throwing the soil out of the ditch with unaccustomed zest. He did not stay long enough, unfortunately, to notice that each shovel-full that Ted scooped out of the ditch he threw with careless abandon over his shoulder so that he filled up the ditch behind as steadily as he cleared it in front.

At that point the poor-law master gave in. Ted was sent to the workhouse where perhaps he could learn to do simple jobs and at least he would have taken his exasperating presence elsewhere to plague other people. Sure enough, it was not long before Ted had stirred up a hornet's nest of controversy, not only in the workhouse but all over the region, on the rights and privileges of a workhouse master over those in his care. It came about when Ted learned, what other inmates probably already knew, that the master was feeding inmates' food to his pony. The master claimed that he was merely disposing of waste food and no serious charge was made against him but the arguments raged so fiercely in some quarters that he found it prudent to get rid of his pony.

For a time after that, Ted rested on his laurels but it was not long before he was in trouble again. It was a failing in Ted to indulge from time to time in footling deeds of law-breaking, and it was particularly exasperating to all concerned that he was always caught at it. It came to be believed that Ted welcomed a spell in Ipswich or Norwich gaols as a respite from the workhouse. Certainly there was a fairly regular shuttle between the two institutions for some years.

'This is the fourteenth time we've seen you,' an Ipswich magistrate told him wearily. 'Well,' answered Ted, 'I'm glad to see you keep your books up to date.'

On a similar occasion at Framlingham a more irascible magistrate officiated. The story goes that the magistrate gave way to his irritation at one point by saying: 'You've got enough brass to make a copper.'

'Praps so,' retorted Ted, 'and I reckon you've got enough

water in yar hid to fill it.'

But such tales do little to explain the whole man that was Ted Kittles. Was he just the village simpleton that many found it convenient to think him? Or a cunning mountebank of infinite laziness as the more uncharitable authorities seemed to believe? But simpletons and mountebanks are quickly forgotten — Kittles was not. His reputation became known over a fair slice of East Anglia and lasted long after his death. No light-weight idiot could achieve that. More likely that he was a natural rebel, as hateful and critical of Bumbledom as his state of life allowed him to be, a village Hampden after all, who could only protest safely behind the shield of an assumed idiocy. Such a fool as he was believed to be could utter truths without sacrificing his head. He was, of course, a loner, for who would risk losing his respectable position in the village for the sake of giving support to such a man?

Perhaps Kittles' only fault was that he came too soon, his spirit chained to the times he lived in. Who can doubt but that he would have fared better in these free-spoken days?

James Chambers —
Compulsive Poet

When James Chambers died in 1828 he was eighty years old. It was a longish life in those days even for the most cossetted levels of society and James Chambers can scarcely be numbered among the social elite. For most of his life he wandered the roads and wrote verses and lived as he could. A proper bed to sleep in or a meal set out upon a table were rare experiences and no more welcome to him than any other sign of interference in his chosen way of life. His dependence, little as it was, lay on the good nature of villagers to whom he declaimed his verses and from them he asked no more than a bed on a heap of straw in a farm building and a handful of bread and cheese to see him on his way. Though one of themselves, he was seen by the untutored as a master of language and grammar beyond any possible accomplishment of their own. All in all, what with the cottagers' generosity and later the assistance of more prominent citizens, James fared as well as he needed. In his endless perambulations of rural East Anglia, it was only the Poor Law officers who objected, having no sympathy for anyone who came into their parish to beg.

James Chambers was born at Soham, in Cambridgeshire, into a large family whose head was a retailer of leather pieces. During the early years of his childhood, the family seems to have lived tolerably well on the income from the business. When it declined, it brought in its train a number of troubles, not least of which was the departure of the leather-seller's wife, James' mother, to more agreeable quarters. A period of some domestic chaos followed this event, which Chambers senior sought to correct, on hearing that his wife had died, by marrying again. Far from ameliorating the situation, this rather hasty solution tended

98

to make it steadily worse since the new mother had children of her own and there were frequent dissensions between the two families and particularly between husband and wife over money shortages. The effect of this unhappy household on James was such that he chose to leave it while still no more than a child. Moreover, he never again willingly joined in any family arrangement. When he quit the house at Soham he quit the whole idea of family life, never returned to his birthplace and exhibited no more than a passing curiosity as to the fate of any of his relatives.

How he lived and what experiences he had during the next few years are not known in detail but there must have been someone among those who befriended him who felt some responsibility for the education of this illiterate boy. No doubt but that he was a good pupil, quick to learn and eager to use the words that he learned, for he emerged as one with a facile pen, a sound knowledge of grammar and, it was said, even a smattering of Latin and Greek. By the age of sixteen he had begun his lonely wanderings, mainly in Suffolk, after having spent a short time unhappily making and selling nets and hawking small pottery goods. Apart from such small enterprises, he seems to have renounced the idea of regular work and indeed was too obsessed with freedom of movement, even of the penurious kind to which he had to submit, to take to the burden of peasant drudgery. For some years, as pauper and ballad-monger, he held to the neighbourhood of Haverhill but at the age of forty-two he left that area for good. Tattered and torn, looking like any other vagrant trudging along the roadside, he set out eastwards across the county.

It was an unfortunate way of life so far as the Poor Law authorities were concerned and there must have been times of desperation for James, knowing that the only way he could obtain relief as a pauper was to return to his native parish of Soham where he was registered. Outside of Soham he was officially an alien and liable to be returned to his native village by the authorities if he should be found begging within the local boundaries. Nevertheless, apart

99

from an occasional enforced sojourn in a workhouse, he survived to wander without too much interference. The workhouse experiences, short though they were, he viewed with a loathing that he recalled often in his verses.

Away from such unpleasantness and walking through the countryside, he was generally welcomed by cottagers when he knocked on their doors and no doubt became a familiar figure over the years. He would compose a verse or construct an acrostic on the spot to please the occupants who belived him to be supremely gifted in these matters. A local wedding or public occasion invariably provided the opportunity for a suitable poem or a new acrostic possibly based on the name of the bride or groom or a village notable. The acrostic was seen as a very clever piece of word-play and the recipient felt immensely flattered and ready enough to reward the literary passer-by. If he could find no immediate occasion for verse he would take his finished poems to sell from door to door. They were usually very crudely printed because his handwriting was almost undecipherable — something that his unknown tutor of early years seems to have overloked.

It is difficult to determine now whether James was a compulsive poet dedicated to his muse at all costs or simply a natural wanderer who found this facility to his advantage. His verses are not memorable, though concise and well-written, for his vision is very limited and often confined to his own immediate situation. A set of verses printed in 1810 at the expense of local personages contain a description of a proposed journey from Ipswich to Woodbridge:

> In April he from Ipswich did retire,
> O'er verdant meads, in such distress of mind;
> Woodbridge to see was his express desire,
> Fondly believing he should friendship find.

James never lost sight of the need for patronage and much of his verse goes on in this strain. The sketchy records of his life indicate that in fact he did not arrive in Woodbridge until three months later. However, this would agree with the wandering, unpredictable manner of his life. Perhaps he

100

strayed by the verdant meads of Bealings or Martlesham and gained enough interest from local people to support him there for a time. When he did arrive in Woodbridge he inevitably set down his impressions in verse:

> Replete with keen remorse and discontent,
> Quite penny-less 'mongst man superb he strayed;
> Contemptuous snubs from cynicks did resent,
> Yet did not quite distrust celestial aid.

Aid came in the more mundane form of subscriptions from some gentlemen of the town, which was to be his base for many years to come. He was provided with a small shack on the barrack-ground just outside the town and in due course must have become a familiar sight — a local 'character'. His own comment on that period comes again in the form of a verse in his usual flowery style:

> At length some gentlemen beneficent,
> Excited by rich grace and love divine,
> To sooth his fears and give his mind content
> To raise a small subscription did incline
> That these plain verses might in print appear.

Grateful as he was to the beneficent gentlemen for their help and interest, he soon came to resent their efforts when they extended attempts to improve his way of life. His own idea of patronage was to be given material aid without too many conditions attached. The gentlemen of Woodbridge, however, decided that they would make a new man of the vagrant poet. He was persuaded to wash, shave and dress in new clothes, his hut was cleaned out and a few pieces of furniture introduced. For a short time James appeared in the streets of the town looking almost unrecognisably civilised. The project was a great success with the benevolent gentlemen who congratulated themselves on the good work they were doing. For James, the transformation gave no pleasure at all. The shilling a week that came with the rejuvenation he considered was very hardly earned. Like an adult Huck Finn, he was uncomfortable and fretful in his new clothes and longed for the freedom of his old life. Only the threat that as a pauper he could be sent back to his native village if he did not agree to conform to respectable standards, kept him spruce and unhappy for a time.

When at last he escaped the gentlemens' ministrations and looked back at the way they had interfered with his chosen style of existence, no matter how well-intentioned their motives, he declared: 'That was the worst day of my life.' Even patronage, he had discovered, demanded its price. Soon, he relapsed into his old ways and was still walking the roads and writing verse until well into his seventies. The inspiration for some of his poems seemed to arrive from bizarre occasions:

Lines on a Black Dog stealing the Author's Meat.

On a Brinded Greyhound carrying a piece of meat to the Author.

On a Maid Servant killing two Cats.

On a gift of coals to the poor by Lady Rowley at Stoke-by-Nayland.

Verses on a Rat knawing Twine and winding it many times around the Bed-post.

As time went on, James wandered farther afield and it was on a bitterly cold day in mid-winter that he appeared like some ancient scarecrow in the village of Stradbroke. There was an unoccupied farmhouse there where he found shelter and the owner allowed him the use of two rooms to rest and recuperate during the bleak weather. It was too late to arrest the effect of cold and exposure upon such an aged body and in a few days he was seriously ill. Two local women were kind enough to look after him, keeping him warm with blankets and hot gruel but this was to be the end of roaming for the old man. He had survived so long the rigours of his hard life but at eighty could withstand it no more. He died within a few days of reaching Stradbroke and left there his worldly possessions — a few scraps of poetry, a bushel of wheat gleaned from the fields and tenpence halfpenny.

Eleanor Short — Scold

The parish of Boulge in Suffolk has an air of peace as profound as anywhere else in this peaceful part of the country. As if some sanctity remained from the long, calm years that the poet, Edward Fitzgerald, spent here, the place maintains a remote tranquillity scarcely disturbed by the visits of literary tourists come to pay their respects at the celebrated tomb.

Yet this same spot — for it is not recognisably a village — once sheltered a formidable character, a woman of such virulent temper that her reputation has survived for over two hundred years. This was the redoubtable Mrs. Eleanor Short, who built the Lodge that Edward Fitzgerald was later to occupy and whose domestic quarrels and caprices were the scandal of the countryside. Apparently thriving on the acute dissensions that characterised her three marriages, the lady then obstinately continued to live as a widow to a ripe old age, against the heartfelt prayers and wishes of many a sufferer under her regime.

Though an extremely wealthy and powerful woman, little is known of her life until a succession of marriages brought consequent changes in her name. Starting out with the maiden name of Martin, she in turn became Mrs. Plummer of Lewes in Sussex, Mrs. William Whitby of Boulge and finally Mrs. Henry Short. To add to the wealth of names, her third husband, who was an Army colonel, had seen fit to change his name from Hassard to Short some time before meeting with the widow of William Whitby. Another member of the family, a niece, also changed her name to Rissowe by marriage and then to Sharpe by choice.

The occupation of the Hall at Boulge by the Shorts impinged upon the more celebrated domestic plans of the Fitzgeralds, since the parents of Edward were hopeful of living there. In fact, they coveted Boulge Hall and its beautiful grounds so intensely that they rented the nearby

Bredfield Hall to live there until old Mrs. Short should die and the house become vacant. However, having never in her life done anything willingly to please others, she was not likely to forgo the pleasure of living as long as possible to spite everyone, including the Fitzgeralds.

When at last the senior Fitzgeralds were able to move into Boulge Hall, Edward decided to occupy the attractive small Lodge within the grounds and no doubt knew that the place had been built by Mrs. Short as a retreat during her years of tantrums with the colonel. If her spirit ever came to disturb the quiet that E.F.G. enjoyed there, he never mentioned it though there are some still so conscious of the old lady's power that they will point out that the Lodge was later completely destroyed by fire.

Mrs. Short often referred to the Lodge as her 'city of refuge' and spent long periods there apart from her husband. Though always regarded as the instigator of all the quarrels at the Hall, there is something defensive in her regular visits to the Lodge that suggests that faults were perhaps not entirely on her side. Certainly, she and her third husband were an ill-matched pair from the start — he at fifty years old with no marital experience and probably set in his ways while she had sailed through two mens' lives already like an imperious queen.

Of her second husband, William Whitby, from whom she inherited Boulge Hall, little is known beyond the information given on a tablet in the parish church. This is expansive on the subject of William's virtues, recorded in a lengthy and rather obscure verse but tells little else except that he died at the age of forty-three. Since Eleanor's first husband must also have died when quite young, there was outspoken suspicion among the minions who knew of Madam's outrageous behaviour that their demise had been hastened by the wear and tear of life with her.

A widow for the second time at the age of forty-five and undisputed mistress of a grand house and estate, she was prepared to embark on another married spell should a suitable husband turn up. It was not long before she met the man destined to share her eccentric existence unhappily for some years to come. He was a modest, soldier-like man, it was said, who had been a Lieutenant-Colonel in the Royal Dragoons and who hailed from Edlington in Lincolnshire. Later, when the situation at the Hall became intolerable, he returned to his native Edlington, probably bitterly regretting that he had ever left its boundaries.

Although the colonel became joint lord of the manor with his wife, it was soon made clear to him his small importance in the household and in the menage generally. His wife controlled all, except her own temper and her unpredictable moods. After the masculine life of a bachelor soldier and the authority of his rank, a domineering matriarchy was the last thing to merit the colonel's admiration and the awkward, painful tug-of-war began.

At that time, and for long after, Eleanor Short became known as the 'Queen of Hell'. It is an odd, dissonant kind of sobriquet that must surely have originated with the unletter-ed servants and estate workers and yet is more than sufficiently convincing as to the kind of person she was. No mere domineering conduct could earn that title for the Shorts were 'gentry' and so qualified to domineer as much as they pleased so long as they paid the wages. Madam's behaviour went far beyond the level of arrogance that humble servants were expected to endure. There were violent tantrums from which no one in the house escaped and fits of destruction succeeded by long sullen silences during which she would glare malevolently at anyone without reason or discrimination. No doubt but that such extremes would also bring out the less agreeable aspects of the colonel's nature and he would be as ready to quarrel or to ignore according to the mood of the day. On occasion they would not only ignore each other but each other's pet animal, so that she would turn her back on his dog while paying effusive attention to her cat. The colonel, in return, would fuss over his dog and kick the cat.

Even after Mrs. Short had had the Lodge built and furnished to her taste, there was only intermittent relief.

Each of the combatants simmered resentfully in their separate residences, either just recovering from a recent fray or preparing some telling barbs for the next. The colonel was heard on more than one occasion to give his opinion that the ancient scold's bridle used in earlier centuries should never have been done away with.

As his wife removed herself periodically to the Lodge, the colonel came to think that it was an example worth following and in a desire to be absent from the Hall as much as possible rather than from a zealous concern for good causes, he assisted manfully in local affairs. Among other offices, he became a steward of the Woodbridge Subscription Society, a post that scarcely required such qualifications as he possessed. On occasion he was called on to serve on the Grand Jury at the Assizes. At the time of Napoleon's threat of invasion, the colonel gallantly enrolled himself as a private in the Suffolk Yeoman Cavalry and also helped in the raising and organising of the militia in local areas. It was some respite for the real battles that occurred on the domestic front.

For all their determined absences, quarrels continued whenever the couple met on common ground. A kind of climax to their differences came around the end of the year and the century, the first of January, 1800, when with New Year guests still present and servants at their last reserves of patience, Mrs. Short made a brief but spectacular attempt to demolish the dining-room. Every object which could be used as a missile was thrown at the windows, all of which were well and truly smashed. There was also some threat that she would set fire to the farm buildings and a rumour that a fire started in the dining-room had burned a hole in the floor. Certainly the colonel and attendant servants were in some concern that the lady should be restrained. Whether or not it was at this point that Mrs. Short produced the knife is not clear, since so much of this story of the domestic rumpus comes from long-ago accounts by word of mouth from a variety of spectators and a host of gossips. There is a haziness about the matter that later caused it to be recorded

106

merely as folk-lore. A contribution by the local historian, Vincent B. Redstone, to a book published in 1893 on rural folk-lore includes this passage:

'Boulge is said to be haunted by a Mrs. Short, who is called the "Queen of Hell". She murdered a gentleman at Boulge Hall. The stain is on the floor where she murdered him. Now, she comes out of the gate in a carriage with a pair of horses that have got no heads. She wears a silk dress. There is a light in the carriage and a man drives the horses. About three years ago a servant girl lived there. The ghost of Mrs. Short went into her room and pulled all her things off her. The girl said she felt the ghost's breath like a wolf upon her.'

So much for the mish-mash collected from gossip and local superstition. However, there are some facts connected with the matter which are on official record. There is no doubt that at some stage, Mrs. Short wielded a knife and was forcibly deprived of it by four male servants. For their pains, they were indicted at Ipswich Quarter Sessions for 'an assault and confinement of Mrs. Short on the 1st of January last, 1800, at Boulge Hall.' The four unfortunate servants, William Walker, Richard Jackson, William Southgate and Sam Baldry, obtained their dismissal after a full knowledge of the situation was taken. The fact that there were so many male servants in attendance seems significant of the conditions at the Hall.

It was the last straw so far as the colonel was concerned. Having made his will, he prepared to leave the Queen of Hell for good. The will expressed his bitter determination that Mrs. Short should not receive a penny from his bequests, most of his possessions going to his brother and a sum of money to the Potter family at Lowestoft to whom he occasionally fled for refuge. In the wording of the will, great care was taken by the colonel 'that no distant contingency may give a claim of right to my wife, Eleanor Short.'

He further directed that he was under no circumstances to be buried at Boulge. The rejection was complete and mutual. Madam at once disposed of everything likely to remind her of the colonel. When he died in 1807 and she became a widow for the third time it was apparently with considerable relief. She was sixty. From that point onwards her reputation as a virago waned and she seems to have taken on a much more tranquil though still wilfull role for another twenty-four years. As a woman with considerable wealth and property to bestow, it was not difficult to entice a favourite great-niece, Mary Ann, to become her companion and support. From the tone of her letters at the time and in her will she obviously displayed to Mary Ann both consideration and affection — blessings given in very short supply to her husbands. 'To my dear and affectionate great-niece Mary Ann Martin Stimson, who lives with me, all my real estate, stocks, funds, money and securities, furniture, glass and plate.'

Everything left to Mary Ann and no doubt richly earned for she stayed with Mrs. Short until the latter died. How difficult it was for her and how critically she must sometimes have balanced the promised inheritance with her own personal freedom during those long years can be judged perhaps by the fact that she married immediately after her great-aunt's death. While she waited and while the Fitzgeralds waited for the old lady to die, one can believe that the former termagent had modified her way of life at least to the point of being merely cantankerous but no longer justifying the title 'Queen of Hell'. It is a bitter name for any human being to carry, deserved or not. But if there was no such title, perhaps there would be no story.

Knight and Squire

A fearsome duel to the death was fought on Cawston Heath in Norfolk at the point known as Woodrow, on the 20th August, 1698. A stone still marks the spot where the two distinguished local gentlemen sought satisfaction for their wounded pride through the incisive certainty of cold, merciless steel. It is said that the encounter was the last to be fought in England but it must be doubted that this is true, although strict new laws now made duelling the sort of contest in which neither side could win. If the bout was not lost by the vulnerability of the flesh then it would be lost, more likely than not, by being arrested for wounding or even for murder. Nevertheless, the concept of gentlemenly honour still prevailed and with it the belief that the only dignified way to rebut a slur that impugned the character was to challenge the misguided slanderer to a duel. That there was nothing to be gained from these encounters except 'satisfaction' makes them appear somewhat absurd and pointless nowadays, since only the law or a bloody sword gained the settlement of the dispute in the end and seems to show that there must have been a considerable degree of pig-headed ritual about the affairs. Often, of course, there was some background of conflict behind the immediate pretext of an insult and in the case of the ill-fated Cawston duel, whose combatants had certainly met on many occasions, the climax arose from a mutual dislike of each other's politics, way of life and simply territorial proximity.

The two men concerned in this insensate quarrel were well-known sons of Norfolk, though there was some difference between their relative status and importance. Oliver Le Neve was a descendant of an ancient family of modest pretensions whose name had been sullied, in some upper-class eyes, by dipping into trade and doing very well out of it. It was from his uncle, a wealthy stationer, that Oliver had inherited a considerable amount of landed property in Norfolk. As befitting the life-style that the inheritance allowed him to follow, Oliver took up resisence at Witchingham Hall in 1692, became a J.P. and a Captain of Militia and generally filled the role expected of a popular squire. His relations with county families of similar status were cordial and he was well-supported by his friends. So far as he was concerned, it was a good life and he had a thoroughly good part to play in it, together with his beautiful wife and lively young family. In politics, his sympathies lay with the exiled Jacobites rather than with the new King William III but he took no active interest in the affairs of either Whigs or Tories.

His adversary in the duel was a much more formidable personality. It was no less, indeed, than Sir Henry Hobart, who had been knighted at the age of thirteen when Charles II came on a visit to the family's seat at Blickling Hall. Despite this personal honour, Sir Henry had no love for the Stuarts and chose instead to espouse the cause of the Whigs new king, in whose hands lay the opportunities of the future.

In appearance, Sir Henry presented an ideal picture of a powerful aristocrat, tall and handsome, with a commanding presence. No doubt such skills as that of swordsmanship had been his from boyhood and in his arduous fencing lessons he had been well-known to express the over-riding ire and impatience that was part of his nature. In any armed encounter, Sir Henry must surely have known that advantage was overwhelmingly on his side. As for other aspects of his life, however exalted and important they may have appeared, they all suffered from one general and worsening malaise — shortage of money. Not only had he inherited vast debts from his father but the shortfall was steadily increasing year by year owing to the heavy cost of his own political ambitions. The erosion of the Hobart estate to pay off creditors was a constant and worrying threat to his self-esteem and position. To stem the losses, he was not above using ruthless methods of squeezing those tenants, neighbours and underlings who were in any way dependent upon him.

110

'I wish,' wrote Humphrey Prideaux, Archdeacon of Suffolk, to a friend, 'Sir Henry, instead of prosecuting his neighbours, would think of paying his debts, which he take no care of, but uses his privilege to protect himself.'

In 1698, another bout of intense and expensive electioneering for the Whig cause and his own advancement, caused a serious draining of the knight's resources but he seemed set on spending every penny likely to help him gain a seat. It was all in vain. Against all custom and prediction the voting went against Sir Henry, who saw his hard work, wealth and ambition disposed of in one blow. He spent the days that followed the defeat closed up at Blickling Hall, pacing up and down like a caged animal and ready to seize upon any excuse to vent his anger. Such an excuse came almost at once when some gossiping crony stated his belief that Sir Henry had lost the election because of rumours put about that he had acted as a coward in the military campaign in Ireland some years before. Incensed, Sir Henry demanded to know the source of such a scurrilous insult and was told that it had originated with Oliver Le Neve. Without a moment's hesitation he issued the challenge. Here was something that impugned his honour and required a quick and violent correction. He would fight a duel with this upstart Tory, Le Neve, if necessary to the death and make an example of him as a lying rogue. It would also provide an outlet for all the frustration he felt about his other misfortunes.

Le Neve receieved the challenge in some surprise and at once wrote back to deny any knowledge of the rumour. By this time, he had married for a second time and was happily engrossed in his accumulating family and his estate. He had no taste for duelling nor indeed any room for unwarrantable animosity and he believed that his firm but friendly repudiation of the slur would end the matter. To a man in a reasonable state of mind this may well have been so but Sir Henry desperately needed a whipping-boy, an object on which he could turn his fury. Rather than accept the denial, he raced down to Reepham on a horse soon lathered in

111

sweat, expecting to find Le Neve there and intending to give himself the pleasure of challenging him to his face. As it happened, Le Neve was away and Sir Henry gained only the savage satisfaction of stating publicly that Le Neve's letter denying knowledge of the slander showed him to be a coward who was trying to squirm out of the fight.

In a sterner mood now, Le Neve wrote again to the baronet. He repeated that he was innocent of the original charge that he was responsible for setting forth rumours but added that since Sir Henry had chosen to believe that he had said so out of cowardice, he had no alternative but to prove otherwise. 'Send me the time and place,' the letter concluded, 'for the matter shall not rest as it is though it cost me my life.'

With a heavy heart Le Neve despatched the letter and at once received notice of a suitable time and place for the duel. As far as possible he set his affairs in order and on the morning of that fateful day said his farewells to his family. It was not likely that he would overcome his expert opponent and in any case had no great stomach for shedding blood.

On Cawston Heath on a bright summer's morning the two men met and hurriedly prepared. Without a word to each other they followed the instructions of their seconds and took up the proper stance with their sword points crossed. On the command, the swords rose and flashed wickedly in the sunlight as each man sought to out-manoevre the other. For Sir Henry, still in a fury of hate, nothing could satisfy him but to engage the other in a ferocious attack that soon had his opponent's arm pierced and heavily bleeding. Desperately aware that he could not long withstand the weakening loss of blood, Le Neve sought strongly to overcome the baronet's experienced guard.

As it happened, Le Neve had a slight advantage here, though he had probably not recognised it as such. He was left-handed, a fortuitous accident of birth that tended to confuse Sir Henry since all his long experience of swordsmanship would undoubtedly be with right-handed opponents. With Le Neve's attacks coming from an unexpected

112

quarter, Sir Henry lost his guard momentarily and allowed the other to find an opening. It was with a dying effort that Le Neve plunged his sword home deep in the baronet's stomach. Then, both men prostrate from their wounds, they were hurried away to be attended by surgeons. Sir Henry died two days later of the fatal wound but Le Neve gradually recovered, only to find himself about to be charged with murder for a duel that he had never wanted and for which there had been no reason. His chief offence lay in killing someone who was important and powerful, with influential followers led by Lady Hobart who were determined on seeking full justice. If Le Neve's opponent had been a humbler man or had the result gone the other way, the law might well have accepted that the affair was justified by long tradition and taken no action. As it was, the prudent thing was to disappear from the scene for a very long time.

Le Neve fled to Holland with the law already on his heels and there he hid his tracks as well as possible by taking a succession of different names and living inconspicuously in modest accomodation that was frequently changed. Amid great secrecy, his friends sometimes made contact, sending gifts and comforting messages for his support. Unfortunately, the forces of vengeance in England, with Lady Hobart at their head, demanded a trial of the absent squire and in due course this came about at the Thetford Assizes. There, it was proclaimed that if Le Neve did not return and surrender to the processes of the law, he would be deemed an outlaw and have to take the consequences.

For something over a year Le Neve stayed exiled in Holland. As time passed, the early whispers of sympathy grew into a clamour, particularly from the vast number of East Anglians on his side. There were other signs, too, that brought hope to the squire. For one thing, the previous Sheriff of Norfolk had been succeeded by a new Sheriff of a much more tolerant attitude. Then there was the rumour that the virulent Lady Hobart had begun to think of marrying again and was in a mind to drop the persecution of her husband's slayer. When he was certain that the climate in England was changing to his advantage, Le Neve came back, at first disguised and under the identity of 'Mr Browne, Sword Cutler', but it was not long before he tired of such an unnatural situation. He wanted to be able to go home to Witchingham and to be able to meet his friends in the open without such cloak-and-dagger subterfuge. Though there were some who shook their heads at his decision, it seemed to him that the best course was to give himself up to the mercy of the courts rather than risk the curse of outlawry. In January, Le Neve attended a hearing at which he was charged to present himself for trial at the Assizes in April. In the interim he was allowed his freedom through the sureties given by his friends. He immediately returned to Witchingham and in the idyllic weeks that followed he spent his time contentedly in the heart of his family, farming and hunting in a familiar routine. With apparent calm he watched the days go by until the date of the dreaded Assizes drew near. Again he said his adieus and presented himself for trial. The court was crowded with friends and well-wishers of the public and it seemed that the Grand Jury too, was inclined to look indulgently on a misdemeanour which had already claimed punishment enough. Without a dissentient, they voted to acquit him of the blame for Sir Henry Hobart's life.

After so long under a cloud which had fundamentally affected the whole of his family's life, Le Neve now hoped no doubt to spend the rest of his life quietly at Witchingham. Unfortunately, this country squire seemed to be one of those to whom the hand of an unhappy fate is ever ready to point. One family tragedy after another disturbed the passing years. Not long after his acquittal, Le Neve's wife died and when in the following year he took another wife she died a few weeks after the marriage. When his only son also died in July 1711, the squire himself soon followed as if glad to be done with a life of misfortunes.

Edward Fitzgerald —
Wanderer

There are many labels that will fit Edward Fitzgerald in part — hardly any that will compass the whole man. He was a poet and scholar and, as everyone knows; the inspired translator of *Omar Khayyam*. He was a countryman but also a sailor; a recluse yet the valued friend of local wits and literary giants; a man who enjoyed the benefits of a wealthy background but was always conscience-stricken about the plight of the poor. Altogether, a complex person of conflicting interests.

Yet there was one trait of Edward Fitzgerald that was undeniably consistent. He confessed to it himself: 'I am a very lazy fellow who do nothing and this is what I have been doing in many different places.' Idle he was throughout his life but it was a meditative idleness in which thoughts were born and no one can have been so idle to better purpose. Allied to his idleness was a simple but consuming curiosity about places and people that led him to wander endlessly over the byways of his beloved country. This was his peculiar eccentricity and the best and most comprehensive description of him and his way of life lies in the tag of 'intellectual vagabond'. Others who knew him have called him a 'genteel gypsy'. His love of the freedom to wander and dawdle and observe prevailed over all. No matter that by birth and upbringing he was a distinguished member of the upper social classes and of the literary intellegentsia, by personal inclination he was a kind of superior tramp. By some contradiction in his nature he was no traveller or explorer of distant parts and constantly rejected invitations to go abroad but was always happy in wandering casually over East Anglian territory that never grew stale to him.

Even as a young man, his visits abroad were rare and usually accompanied by a panic desire to get home again quickly. To be sure he seemed to enjoy the holiday he spent in Paris with his friend Thackeray and there were a few occasions when he could be persuaded to go to Ireland to visit a relative but his anxiety to exchange the distant view for more familiar haunts always marked his stay. When he visited Wales in 1833 he returned by stage coach, travelling almost non-stop for two days to reach London.

His wanderings in this country, on the other hand, were leisurely and completely happy. Wherever he went it was with the precious freedom to stand and stare and to disdain time-tables. When young he had roamed extensively throughout England but in more mature years he had his favourite places to go to and people to see. It was Cambridge at first that called him back after leaving the University and he returned there regularly for many years. He loved to be there in the spring, to stroll around and see old friends. He would take for as long as the charm remained for him, sometimes for a whole term. In London he wandered about with the same unhurried curiosity from bookshop to art gallery or in the evening from pot-house to opera. Time was his servant and never his master. After a time, when such visits had satisfied his constant wonderment, he would be happy to get back again to Suffolk and his home at Boulge.

Ever since the beginning of his student days, Fitzgerald had managed to separate himself domestically from his family, not from any real differences but because he recognised his own paramount need for personal freedom. When the family had moved to Boulge Hall, therefore, Edward at once looked around for a suitable separate dwelling for himself and found it almost ideally in a small thatched house within the grounds — the Lodge, as it was called. It would do very well for a temporary home, he thought, and it remained 'temporary' for the whole of the sixteen years that he lived there.

Boulge was never a very exciting place and he was often critical of the monotony. 'One of the dullest places in England,' he considered. But in fact he entertained frequently when at home and when the loneliness became oppressive he would be off again on his meanderings.

'I am now returned to my dull home after pottering about in the midland counties,' he wrote. He did not often go so far and, whether dull or not, he usually pottered much closer to Boulge. When the Tennysons went to live in Italy they tried to persuade Fitzgerald to join them there. While half-envying their enjoyment of a foreign sun, he could not bring himself to leave these shores.

'Say as you will,' he wrote to them, 'there is not nor ever was such a country as Old England. I am sure no travel would carry me to any land so beautiful as the good sense, justice and liberality of my countrymen make this. And I cling the closer to it because I feel that we are going down the hill.'

So, instead of Italy's wonders, he contented himself with browsing around his usual visiting places in East Anglia. His friend W. B. Donne commented that Fitzgerald haunted the same places at similar seasons of the year so regularly he must regard himself as a plant or a ghost.

Fitzgerald's favourite visiting place for many years was Geldeston, near Beccles, where his sister lived and where he found the most perfect conditions for idle contemplation. Long summer days beside the Waveney produced who-knows-what thoughts to be recollected later when in a writing mood. Of practical things, the only achievement was in learning to swim there. An indulgent sister and an assortment of nephews and nieces made his sojourns at Geldeston always longer and happier than he expected.

When he felt it was time to move on to other pastures, it would likely be to Donne's home at Mattishall or to the even more tempting prospect of a few weeks as a guest of his great friend W. K. Browne. Here, at Bedford, he loved to wander without any concern as to time or social commitments along the quiet valley of the Ouse. 'It is all deuced pleasant,' he wrote. 'In half an hour I shall go to the village two miles off and fish and have tea in a pot-house and so walk home. For all of which idle ease I think I shall be damned.'

117

The matter of unfair privilege bothered him sometimes and he compensated for his feelings of guilt by siding strongly with the cottage poor against the wrongs of the new-style, money-conscious squires whom he despised. It seemed to Fitzgerald that they no longer accepted their responsibility for the welfare of the village people nor cared enough for the countryside itself. He frequently raised his voice in indignation at the arbitrary felling of trees and the blocking of time-honoured footpaths.

After an enjoyable spell at Bedford — where next? Perhaps to his study at Boulge for a time before setting out again, often on the spur of the moment. These were the wanderings he loved most, where he was completely free and vagabond-ish, unaware of anything beyond his absorbing interest in the country and its people. Sometimes he seemed to be unaware even of his destination.

'How did I get here?' he wrote from Lowestoft in 1841. 'Why, I left Geldeston yesterday to go to Norwich. Then I expected Donne to carry me back to Mattishall. No Donne came so after sitting seven hours in the Commercial Room I got up on the coach by which I had set out and vowed I would not get out till it stopped. It stopped here by the sea — I was satisfied. I felt that it could not reasonably be expected to go further — so here I have spent the day. Like a naughty schoolboy I won't go home to Geldeston just yet.'

This account is light-hearted enough but gives some idea of the delays and difficulties of travel and communication at that time — none of which seem to have deterred this inveterate rover. Occasionally however, his disregard of creature comforts on these unplanned excursions had disagreeable effects. He was feeling ill, he once complained, because he had been walking too long in the sun, then eaten too many unripe peaches and then gone to sleep lying in long, wet grass.

When his brother moved into Boulge Hall, Edward Fitzgerald followed his usual course of keeping a healthy gap between himself and his family by giving up the Lodge and moving in with the Smith's who kept a farm at Farlingaye

Hall, on the edge of Woodbridge. Later, he took lodgings on the Market Hill with a gunsmith named Berry.

This, too, was only intended to be a temporary arrangement but in fact Fitzgerald spent thirteen contented years at this address and was only persuaded to move when Mr Berry's new wife indicated that she was not in favour of lodgers. Fitzgerald had enjoyed living in the centre of what activity and bustle the little town had to offer and making friends with an assortment of tradespeople and workmen. When literary friends from London came to pay their respects they were usually lodged at the nearby Bull Hotel. The condition of his two rooms at Berry's made entertaining there not only cramped but hopelessly cluttered, with odds and ends like the junk to be found in a second-hand shop. One of these items was a multi-coloured mop which stood against his wall and which he would not allow to be used in the kitchen.

Another advantage of living on the Market Hill at Woodbridge was that he could easily stroll down to the river and his yacht, *the Scandal*, anchored in the Deben. There the sense of freedom was perfect and he would spend long summer days on the boat. His love of ships and the sea and the kind of independent mariner to be found along the East Anglian coast took him off frequently on journeys to Lowestoft and Aldeburgh and when Carlyle came to see him it was immediately to Aldeburgh that he took the great man.

So important was the freedom to wander and contemplate throughout Fitzgerald's life that his unfortunate and short-lived marriage came only as an ill-judged interruption. In no time at all he had returned to his old haunts, his old friends, his old clothes and was happy again. As the years passed, his roaming became more circumscribed but not less frequent. 'What a lazy beast I am for not going to Ireland', he wrote with regard to an invitation from Thackeray.

The wonder of photography came in time to capture the 'likeness' of Edward Fitzgerald but a more illuminating picture comes from the description given by a contemporary. He remembered 'an old gentleman wandering, or rather drifting abstractedly about the country roads in an ill-fitting suit with a shabby hat on the back of his head, blue spectacles on nose and an old cape cast anyhow about his shoulders. Few figures were more familiar to me by sight, few less regarded; and many a time must my pony's hoofs have spattered this forlorn-looking figure as we cantered past him in neighbouring lanes.'

For over twenty years Fitzgerald had vacillated over the purchase of a 'permanent' home and the quest for a perfect site had often been the excuse for further jaunts into the countryside. In the end he concluded that he could do worse than stay in the town he knew and loved best. A likely property in a quiet road was purchased and altered to his instructions and eventually came to be known as Little Grange. For some reason he seemed to have no great fondness for the place and even when his accommodation at Berry's came to an end, he was reluctant to enter his new home. Instead, he tried to extend the familiar tenor of his years at Berry's by taking rooms next door but this was by no means so cosy and he had to cater for himself. Like a naughty schoolboy again, he continued his truancy from Little Grange by making lengthy visits to Lowestoft. It was not until the spring of 1874 that he eventually moved into his new house, remarking moodily that this was probably where he would die.

Much more appropriately, it was on one of his rounds of the countryside that his life was peacefully concluded. For the last time he had thrown himself upon the hospitality of W. B. Donne at Mattishall, almost the only one left of his earlier friends and in that house of so many happy memories Fitzgerald retired to sleep and did not wake again.

Other titles published by Barbara Hopkinson Books

SUFFOLK IN COLOUR — Barbara Hopkinson
46 full colour illustrations with accompanying text.

THE SUFFOLK WE LIVE IN — Paul Fincham
A clear, concise and beautifully illustrated outline of the county's
long life and varied fortunes.

SUFFOLK TALES — H. Mills West
A collection of short stories of days gone by.

EAST ANGLIAN TALES — H. Mills West
28 short stories of rural life fifty or so years ago.

MARDLES FROM SUFFOLK — Ernest R. Cooper
A taste of East Anglian humour.

GHOSTS OF EAST ANGLIA — H. Mills West
22 ghost stories old and new.

A SUFFOLK CHILDHOOD — Simon Dewes
Memories of Hadleigh from 1914 to 1919.